Shannon Ansted Hake

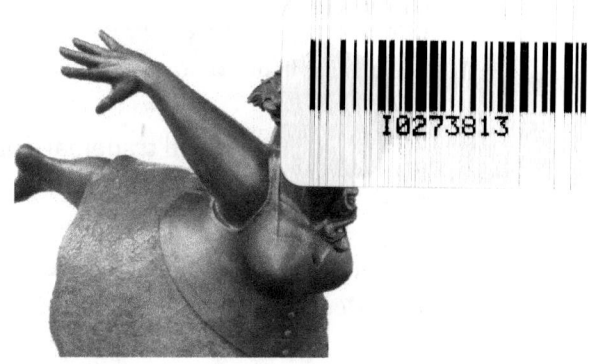

I Am Beautiful

Heal Your Life,
One Day at a Time

Published by
SHANNON HAKE
Since 2013

Fort Collins

I Am Beautiful

Copyright © 2012- present by Shannon Ansted Hake

All Rights Reserved.
Published in the United States by Shannon Hake.

Shannon Hake is a registered trademark of Shannon Hake, Healing Touch, LLC.

The author of this book is not a physician. Nothing in here is intended to prescribe, diagnose or otherwise give medical advice. Please consult your medical practitioner as needed.

ISBN 978-0-9913084-0-8 (softcover)

Ansted Hake, Shannon 1968-
I Am Beautiful / by Shannon Ansted Hake.

Bronze sculpture by James Lynxwiler,
www.lynxwiler.com.
Photo by Shannon Hake.
Photo editing by Dave Hake.

Any portion of this book may be reproduced, stored in a retrieval system, or transmitted in any form or by any means – electronic, mechanical, photocopy, recording, scanning, or any other – as long as you state where it came from. This book is meant to create momentum and identify a few tools for your own healing process.

As much as I would love to guarantee results, those are really up to you. What you get out of this depends on the consistency, diligence and actions of yourself.

I Am Beautiful

This book is dedicated:

To my children Tucker, Finn and Ayanna; who have been with me through thick and thin and love me anyway, I love you anyway, too.

To my husband Dave; thank you for teaching me how to laugh and continuing to be my steady rock.

To my MS, Louise L. Hay and her book *You Can Heal Your Life*, without which I would not have started my healing journey.

To my mom who spent time with me and the kids after my diagnosis. I don't know what I would have done without your help, thank you, Mom. Thank you, also, for taking the time to catch all the errors that neither I nor my computer caught. Hugs!

To my dad who has always been here for me- helping financially and emotionally when times have been tough, thank you, Dad.

To Cathy White who went to the doctor with me for my MRI. Thank you for giving me loving support while I was learning how to give myself an injection.

To Tracy Brenner who gave me a copy of information for my blood type. Thank you also for the vitamins and minerals. Both have been a huge part of my healing process.

To Lori Rebman who brought me the book by Louise Hay that started me on my healing journey. Thank you, Lori.

To Ashley Cranor who has also been with me through easy and difficult. Thank you for your love, kindness and support throughout the years, love you.

I love you all with every ounce of my being.

I Am Beautiful

Contents

January 8
February 39
March 68
April 99
May 129
June 160
July 190
August 221
September 252
October 282
November 313
December 343
Resources 374

I Am Beautiful

Preface

I AM BEAUTIFUL... If reading this title you think to yourself, "No, I'm not," then this book is for you. If you think, "How arrogant!" this book is for you. If you had any other thought than, "Yes, I am", this book is intended for you.

There is nothing in your life more powerful than your thoughts. If you pay attention, you'll begin to see how those thoughts create your days. Everything in your life is a product of a thought you've had somewhere along the way.

Since the one person you are always with is YOU – make sure you love yourself.

I Am Beautiful

INTRODUCTION

When I first started writing this book it was just for me, as a healing guide. I wrote it as a reminder to live life in a positive light. I had recently been diagnosed with Multiple Sclerosis and knew I needed to examine things. A friend brought me Louise Hay's book, *You Can Heal Your Life*. It had a profound impact on how I looked at myself. I realized I didn't like myself, let alone love myself. When I started looking at people around me, I realized others needed to love themselves as well. It was time to make a change. Changing my thinking has changed my life.

You'll see I wrote it mostly in the first person because that's how I talk to myself. It's how I focus my thoughts. This writing is a daily reminder to see beauty inside, as well as outside of yourself.

A big piece of using this book is to take the *"Thought for the Day"* and really immerse yourself in it. Copy it down on a piece of paper and post it somewhere you look often. Say the thoughts over and over and over again. Create your own *Thought for the Day* if you don't like mine. Watch your life change into something positive – something more of what you really want.

Here's a small example of how this works: One day I was feeling sad – downright blue. I looked at the clock and it said 1:11. I knew from previously reading books by Dr. Doreen Virtue that the Universe was about to take a snapshot of my thoughts. I immediately said, "I am happy, healthy, wealthy, safe, grounded and free." My attitude changed at once. I felt lighter, less sad, like I could tackle whatever was bothering me.

I Am Beautiful

Your thoughts may seem simple and unimportant. They're not. They have the most power for creating the life you wish to live. Really, since we can't stop them, we might as well learn to make them into useful tools.

You'll also see I left some space after the "*Thought for the Day*". This is for anything you'd like to write down; lists, thoughts, dreams, drawings, memories, realizations, quotes, anything at all. This book is meant to be written in, referenced, and carried around.

As you develop a new relationship with yourself and the world around you, be gentle with yourself. You are amazing and beautiful!

JANUARY

January 1

I am beautiful. Today is a perfect day to take 5 minutes and write my hopes and dreams for this coming New Year. I will focus on what I want. I will be honest and gentle with myself.

Thought for the Day:

I bring new ideas and new energy to this day and all days to come.

I Am Beautiful

January 2

I am beautiful. What did you wake up thinking? Did you wake up happy and giving thanks for another day? Or did you wake up grumpy with negative thoughts about your day?

Pay attention to your thoughts as you go through your day. Just notice what you think. "As you focus on, so shall you manifest."- Rev. Margarita Wind. If you focus on the negative, that's what you'll create. If you focus on the positive, that's what you'll create. Which one do you want in your life?

Thought for the Day:

I am gentle and happy with myself.

I Am Beautiful

January 3

I am beautiful. I awaken to the sounds of my gratefulness running through my head. I am happy to be alive. I am pleased to have another day to live what I was brought here to do.

Thought for the Day:

I give my all in everything I do.

I Am Beautiful

January 4

I am beautiful. Today is a new day to make good choices for myself. I choose to make this time the best I can and live each moment. I know I can only make decisions now, since later doesn't exist.

Ralph Waldo Emerson once said, "This time, like all times, is a very good one, if we but know what to do with it."

Thought for the Day:

Now is the only time.

I Am Beautiful

January 5

I am beautiful. What a lovely day with geese flying overhead in a clear blue sky. Sounds of their honking remind me they encourage each other as they fly. We need to encourage each other too as we fly through our days.

Thought for the Day:

I give the best of myself.

I Am Beautiful

January 6

I am beautiful. Today, no matter what seems chaotic in my life, I will be grounded in the center of myself. If I feel myself getting sucked into negative chaos, I will take a step back and observe. I will remember that I choose my own thoughts.

Thought for the Day:

I am calm, centered and happy.

I Am Beautiful

January 7

I am beautiful. Today is a good day to be aware of the beauty around me. The birds are singing, the sun is shining, and the sky is clear. I am grateful to have my eyesight and other senses to experience it.

Thought for the Day:

I enjoy being alive.

I Am Beautiful

January 8

I am beautiful. When I open my eyes for the first time each day, I say thank you for another day to be me. Today I will set aside some time to just sit. I will close my eyes and focus on my breath. When I am done, I will take time to stretch my body, slowly, thoughtfully. I will pay attention to myself, and listen to my inner voice.

Thought for the Day:

I take time to feed my soul.

I Am Beautiful

January 9

I am beautiful. Today I will focus on positive self-talk. I will post at least one message I want to remember. I can post it in my car, by the phone, or above the toilet paper roll in the bathroom. I will start with one thought I'd like to keep in mind throughout the day.

Thought for the Day:

I am the only me and I love who I am.

I Am Beautiful

January 10

I am beautiful. What a crisp day it is. The sun is shining and clouds are rolling across the sky. Geese are feeding in the grass. It's a beautiful day to feed yourself good thoughts. Since our thoughts create our reality, think what you want. Be patient for old, negative thoughts to quit creating, so new ones can begin to create a new reality.

Thought for the Day:

I am happy, healthy and free.

I Am Beautiful

January 11

I am beautiful. Today is a good day to look in the mirror and smile at you. I don't mean smile on the outside. I mean smile from the inside. Really see your beauty. If you find it challenging to do this, practice throughout the day. Look in the mirror and smile with your eyes. Look at yourself tenderly, as if you are looking at a lover.

Thought for the Day:

I love myself completely.

I Am Beautiful

January 12

I am beautiful. Today the clouds are dark, purplish blue and the trees are bare with their branches reaching out and away from their core. They look so amazing against the darkened sky. Like the trees, I have branches of myself reaching out for expression.

Thought for the Day:

I embrace the many gifts I have.

I Am Beautiful

January 13

I am beautiful. What a calm, lovely day it is. I feel the sun shining on my face, so warm and bright. I close my eyes and breathe deeply; in through my nose and out slowly through my mouth. I breathe in love for myself and breathe out any negativity. I take at least five minutes to experience this calm and love before I start my day.

Thought for the Day:

I honor the Higher Consciousness that flows through me.

I Am Beautiful

January 14

I am beautiful. Today I will be grateful for food I have to eat, the house I live in, and the body I was given. I will look at my life and focus on what I have.

Thought for the Day:

I am grateful for every moment.

I Am Beautiful

January 15

I am beautiful. Really, I am. So was Dr. Martin Luther King, Jr. This day in 1929 is the actual day he was born. He was dedicated to equality of all men and women. He was dedicated to peace and love. Peace and love of yourself is where it all begins. If you can look in the mirror and really love yourself, you'll be able to look at others and really love them.

Thought for the Day:

I have courage and fortitude to do what's right for me.

I Am Beautiful

January 16

I am beautiful. Our bodies are amazing, being able to repair themselves. If we cut our finger, the skin will heal itself. If we get a cold, we'll get better. It doesn't matter what the affliction, our bodies can and will heal themselves if we want them to and believe.

Thought for the Day:

I see beauty in my body and can heal any wound.

I Am Beautiful

January 17

I am beautiful. I love it when the moon is still up as the sun rises. It helps me appreciate the natural beauty this world offers every day.

Thought for the Day:

I see love and beauty everywhere.

I Am Beautiful

January 18

I am beautiful. This is a good day to buy yourself some fragrant flowers and place them in your home. Find a place you walk by often. Every time you notice them, lean over and smell – enjoy their fragrance and their loveliness. The same applies to stopping and enjoying the beauty outside. Just sit in your car or the grass before you enter your workplace. See how the sun changes minute by minute. Take five minutes to watch shadows on the trees.

Thought for the Day:

I am as beautiful as the sun.

I Am Beautiful

January 19

I am beautiful. What a great "nesting" day. Clouds are covering the whole sky like a thick comforter. Today feels like a good day to get grounded, do some baking, cleaning and reflecting.

Thought for the Day:

I am grounded and at peace with myself and my circumstances.

I Am Beautiful

January 20

I am beautiful. Today is a clear, crisp day. The ground is covered in snow, the sun is shining and the air feels clean and cool. It is a great day to let go of worries and fears and send them to the Universe. This is not always an easy task, but many times must be done. Letting go helps me remember to trust the process of life.

Thought for the Day:

I have strength and courage to do what needs to be done.

I Am Beautiful

January 21

I am beautiful. Today is a lovely day to listen to your gut feelings. Quiet your mind and truly listen. In questions of your mind or your gut senses, listen to your gut. It may not make sense. You may not understand why you need to say or do something. Listen anyway.

Thought for the Day:

I have faith and trust in myself.

I Am Beautiful

January 22

I am beautiful. There is nothing like spending time with people you enjoy, doing things you enjoy. Time is a gift. Life is a gift. It's worth taking time to evaluate those who you love and commit to spending time with them. There is hardly anything more precious than this.

Thought for the Day:

I give the gift of my time today.

I Am Beautiful

January 23

I am beautiful. I am so grateful to have another day to work on my thoughts, making them positive and life changing. When things around me seem chaotic, I will remember I only have control of me and my thoughts.

Thought for the Day:

I am happy and healthy.

I Am Beautiful

January 24

I am beautiful. It is important to ask for help when you need it. No matter how big or small, if you ask for help, you will get it.

Thought for the Day:

I have faith in Life.

//
I Am Beautiful

January 25

I am beautiful. The choices you make today affect the rest of your life. Today is a good day to act on something you've wanted to change. A good way to start is by paying attention and changing your thoughts to what you want. For example, "My office is clutter free". Write the thoughts and post them somewhere you look often. It will help you find the motivation to take one step at a time toward what you want changed.

Thought for the Day:

Everything I do, I do with gentleness and love.

I Am Beautiful

January 26

I am beautiful. Today is good day to be thankful for what you have. It's a day to love, live and laugh. Even though there are daily challenges and stressors, it's important to remember what keeps you grounded. If you don't know what keeps you grounded, it's time to find out. Knowing is only the first step. The second step is to make sure you do those things on a daily basis, regardless of what life deals you.

Thought for the Day:

I breathe in beauty and breathe out stress.

I Am Beautiful

January 27

I am beautiful. This morning I remembered to do my stretching. I had only a little bit of time, but I did it anyway. It started my day off so well. It is something that makes me feel beautiful and centered.

Thought for the Day:

I am powerful and beautiful just as I am.

I Am Beautiful

January 28

I am beautiful. Today is a good day to settle in and get some things done around the house. The sky is blanket-like, asking me to slow down and be OK with what is. I have peace knowing that no matter what happens, I am who I am. I am strong. I take a deep breath through my nose and exhale slowly through my mouth.

Thought for the Day:

I am Love, Light and Strength.

January 29

I am beautiful. Today I will clean house. Cleaning house doesn't necessarily mean getting out the vacuum. Cleaning physically may not be an issue, but cleaning mentally, emotionally, or spiritually might be. Today is a good day to reflect and see what needs to be put back in order.

Thought for the Day:

I am organized, clear and happy.

I Am Beautiful

January 30

I am beautiful. Nothing more to say.

Thought for the Day:

I love myself as I am in this moment.

I Am Beautiful

January 31

I am beautiful. Today is a good day to be humble and grateful for all things helping me grow; daily challenges, emotional challenges, things stretching my heart, spiritual challenges, experiences helping me remember to ask for help.

Thought for the Day:

I have love in my heart and can face any challenge.

February

February 1

I am beautiful.   Today the clouds have varying degrees of purples and blues. As I remember to breathe in through my nose and out through my mouth, I get calmer on the inside. I remember to slow down and see beauty everywhere I look.

Thought for the Day:

I remember to breathe and feel my beauty.

I Am Beautiful

February 2

I am beautiful. It makes me feel good to do things for other people; to help them take care of their needs. When I put a smile on someone's face, I put a smile in my heart. I can't help but feel beautiful on the outside when I feel happy on the inside.

Thought for the Day:

I carry kindness and peace wherever I go.

I Am Beautiful

February 3

I am beautiful. Sometimes things happen over which you have no control. It's important to remember how many things over which you do have control; what you eat for breakfast, what you drink throughout the day, what you think. If you make good choices, you can have a clear conscience knowing you did your best for today.

Thought for the Day:

I make good choices for myself.

February 4

I am beautiful. Today I slowed down to look at my priorities. It helps me feel better when I get them in line. It's important for me to spend time connecting with friends, family, animals and plants, taking care of my soul and taking care of my body. What are your top priorities?

Thought for the Day:

I love myself and those around me.

I Am Beautiful

February 5

I am beautiful. People and animals in your life can bring you much joy. Why not let those whom you love, know it? Play with your pets, call a parent or child, even write a short note to someone. Every moment is precious and needs to be treated like that.

Thought for the Day:

I show others I love them by sharing my time.

I Am Beautiful

February 6

I am beautiful. In a moment of frustration, I blurted out, "I don't care!" But realizing what came out, I corrected it and said, "That's not true. I do care, I care deeply. That's why I am so frustrated." How often do we say things we don't mean? It's never too late to examine ourselves and make changes.

Thought for the Day:

I forgive myself and make real changes.

I Am Beautiful

February 7

I am beautiful. This morning, after talking to some friends in the coffee shop, I remembered a couple things. One, it is important what we put into our bodies physically. Two, it is important what we put into our bodies mentally. Our thoughts create, as does the food from which our cells are made. As people on this planet, we have a responsibility to be aware – to think – to create our lives the way we want them.

Thought for the Day:

I create my day by the choices I make.

I Am Beautiful

February 8

I am beautiful. It's a good day to take care of myself. I realized yesterday I was trying to juggle too many things for the following morning - this one. When I decided to ask for help and delegate one of those things, a weight was lifted. All of a sudden, the work load was shared, and I was calmer. What a gift it is to ask for help. What a gift it is for those who you ask.

Thought for the Day:

I ask for help and I get it.

I Am Beautiful

February 9

I am beautiful. If you wake up with the attitude that you will have a great day, you'll have a great day. Today is a good day to focus on positive thoughts. Thoughts are as powerful as any physical action. They are impartial too. If you think positive thoughts, that's what you'll get. If you think negative thoughts, that's what you'll get. It's Universal Law. (Abraham-Hicks)

Thought for the Day:

I am happy, healthy, safe, wealthy and free.

February 10

I am beautiful. I awakened this morning to a blanket of white across my yard and car. Snow is such a gentle, simple gift. Snow not only lightens my space, but also lightens my mood. There is something amazing and special about snow. It helps me realize I am beautiful just as I am. I was made just right, and I am to remember that and be grateful.

Thought for the Day:

I am at peace and full of beauty.

I Am Beautiful

February 11

I am beautiful. This day is spectacular. I awoke today to five more inches of beautiful snow. It's amazing how it transforms the world into a magical place. It lightens things up, washes them off, and renews. Snow reminds me of my beauty, and just how small, yet exquisite I am.

Thought for the Day:

I am balanced, loved, happy and thoughtful.

I Am Beautiful

February 12

I am beautiful. Another nesting day - The sky is gray and white, blanket-like. There is snow falling in dainty, dust-like flakes. It's a great day to move slowly and pay attention to my thoughts and actions. It is a beautiful day to focus on one's own inner beauty and nourish oneself with good food, good thoughts and good company.

Thought for the Day:

I allow myself to move slowly and be beautiful starting from the inside.

I Am Beautiful

February 13

I am beautiful. The first thing I do when I open my eyes is say thank you for another day to be here, another day to do my best. Even on days like this, when I wake up with a head-ache, I am happy to have the challenge of having a good day anyway.

Thought for the Day:

I am precious and cherish myself.

I Am Beautiful

February 14

I am beautiful. Today the sky is blue, air is crisp, birds are singing and geese are feeding on the lawn. It's a great day to be grateful for what I have. I'm thankful for trees that grace my yard. Their bark is so intricate and adds beauty for my eyes to see and hands to touch.

Thought for the Day:

I love myself and others - I am at peace.

I Am Beautiful

February 15

I am beautiful. I realize there is a difference between being positive with hopefulness, and positive with obliviousness. I can take only so much negativity. Just because I choose to be positive and create my world in that light, does not mean I ignore the negative things. I know they are there. I know negative people are in this world. I send those people and those situations good thoughts of healing. I choose not to live there.

Thought for the Day:

I am a source of healing for myself and all other beings.

I Am Beautiful

February 16

I am beautiful. When I look in the mirror, I love what I see. I take good care of myself physically, spiritually, emotionally and mentally. I am perfect just the way I am today. I will walk tall and be proud to be me. If a negative thought comes my way, I will acknowledge it's there and let it go.

Thought for the Day:

I am happy to be me.

I Am Beautiful

February 17

I am beautiful. Today I trust the Universe will bring me good things. I will carefully listen for intuitive whispers to give me direction.

Thought for the Day:

I listen and trust my quiet inner voice.

I Am Beautiful

February 18

I am beautiful. Today I will focus on being kind to other people and look for someone to help. I will go out of my way to be kind to someone I usually wouldn't even talk to. If I start getting sucked into thinking a harsh thought about someone or making fun of people different than me, I will stop. I will put myself in their shoes.

Thought for the Day:

I am kind to everyone.

I Am Beautiful

February 19

I am beautiful. I will focus today on being open-minded to other people's ideas. It does not mean I have to change my ideas; just that I am willing to listen to someone else's point of view.

Thought for the Day:

I open my ears to listen to others.

I Am Beautiful

February 20

I am beautiful. Today I will trust that all my needs will be met. I will remember to breathe in through my nose and out through my mouth. I will relax in my unknowingness.

Thought for the Day:

I trust that all is well.

I Am Beautiful

February 21

I am beautiful. Today I will be the best me I possibly can. I will walk and talk with my head held high and know I am special.

Thought for the Day:

I am unique and incredible.

I Am Beautiful

February 22

I am beautiful. Today's date is a special one, 222. These numbers mean that "Your newly planted ideas are beginning to grow into reality." -Doreen Virtue. Thoughts you have been planting in yourself are starting to sprout and grow wings. These numbers mean, keep going.

Thought for the Day:

I love myself and keep growing.

I Am Beautiful

February 23

I am beautiful. Today I will look for ways we are all connected. I will look to see beauty in everything that has life; from birds to earthworms to soil and seeds that provide our food.

Thought for the Day:

I am connected in some way to everything.

February 24

I am beautiful. Today I will think of the life I want to create for myself. I will think lovingly of myself and those around me. I will also be present in each and every moment.

Thought for the Day:

My thoughts today create tomorrow's tomorrow.

I Am Beautiful

February 25

I am beautiful. Today is my day to be who I want. I will live in the moment as if I have already achieved my goal. If my goal is to see my true beauty, I will walk through my day as if I believe I'm beautiful.

Thought for the Day:

I am strong, kind and beautiful.

I Am Beautiful

February 26

I am beautiful. Today I will focus on my strengths. I will make a list of things I do well. I will appreciate myself for what I can contribute.

Thought for the Day:

I am talented and confident. I feel good about myself.

I Am Beautiful

February 27

I am beautiful. I am important and have worth. I have a unique place in this world that no one else has. I will remind myself of this often as I walk through my day.

Thought for the Day:

I am unique and worthy of good things.

I Am Beautiful

February 28

I am beautiful. I will be strong in my integrity. If I hear someone say negative things about others. I will not join in.

Thought for the Day:

What I say about others, I say about myself.

I Am Beautiful

February 29

I am beautiful. Today I will make a list of 3 things I want to change about my life. I will pick one on which to focus.

Thought for the Day:

I can do this. I can make changes I want in my life.

March

March 1

I am beautiful. Today, crocuses are blooming, the sun is shining, wind is blowing and the sky is clear, crystal blue. This world is coming back to life after a long winter. It's a great day to commit to doing something good for you. It could be eating healthy, choosing to exercise, or thinking good thoughts.

Thought for the Day:

I am committed to improving myself.

I Am Beautiful

March 2

I am beautiful. Today I will move slowly through the world and watch myself as if I am standing next to me. I will speak slowly, gently and remember to breathe.

Thought for the Day:

I am gentle, loving and caring.

I Am Beautiful

March 3

I am beautiful. Today I will remember that everything is perfect just the way it is. I will breathe deeply from my belly and relax.

Thought for the Day:

I am beautiful and love myself just the way I am.

I Am Beautiful

March 4

I am beautiful. Today I will write down 10 things I do well. I will think of things as simple as being helpful to my family or making my neighbor smile. If I struggle to find 10, I will be patient. I will breathe deeply and ask for help opening my eyes to the beauty inside myself.

Thought for the Day:

I am good at many things.

I Am Beautiful

March 5

I am beautiful. I am going to look at myself today in a new light. I will see myself as a beautiful person, not prettier and not uglier than anyone else.

Thought for the Day:

I am beautiful and feel good about myself.

I Am Beautiful

March 6

I am beautiful. Today I will pay attention to negative thoughts that go through my head. When I notice a negative thought, I will acknowledge it and then change it to something positive.

Thought for the Day:

I can do this.

I Am Beautiful

March 7

I am beautiful. The weather today is incredible. Snow is coming down and the air feels warm. It's a wet snow, perfect moisture for my plants. I will choose a positive thought about everything and everyone I see today.

Thought for the Day:

I love things I see in me.

I Am Beautiful

March 10

I am beautiful. Today is the first day of the rest of my life. I am going to live each second with this knowing. I will pay attention to my breath and take each moment as it comes.

Thought for the Day:

I trust myself to make good choices from one moment to the next.

I Am Beautiful

March 11

I am beautiful. Today I will look back at the list I made on February 29th. I will assess how I am doing on the first two changes and start working on the 3rd. If I didn't make a list (because it's not a Leap Year), I will think of one thing I want to change in my life and focus on that.

Thought for the Day:

I am only changing my thoughts. I am O.K. just the way I am.

I Am Beautiful

March 12

I am beautiful. I will remember to breathe and look for beauty inside everyone with whom I come in contact. I will look in their eyes and see the spark of life and love. As Byron Katie said, "What I think about you is who I am."

Thought for the Day:

I am beautiful. You are beautiful. He is beautiful. She is beautiful. We are all beautiful, just the way we are.

I Am Beautiful

March 13

I am beautiful. Today is a good day to reflect on all I have.

I have my eyesight, my hearing, my breath and my legs. I can feel and walk, even if it's in a wheel chair. I have friends and family. I have another day to be alive.

Thought for the Day:

I live in gratitude for all I have.

I Am Beautiful

March 14

I am beautiful. The birds are singing and the sun is shining. I took time to stretch my body and play with my dog. Today I'm going to pay extra attention to my thoughts. I'm going to change every noticed negative thought into a positive one. An example is, "that was dumb of me", changed to, "Oooo, I'll do better next time". This sounds so simple, yet when I actually pay attention it's harder than I think.

Thought for the Day:

I am happy, centered and focused on the positive.

I Am Beautiful

March 15

I am beautiful. Today I will write down 10 things I like about myself. I won't let myself do any less than ten. I will pick one or two to focus on throughout the day and watch how it boosts my self-esteem.

Thought for the Day:

I easily find things that I like about myself.

I Am Beautiful

March 16

I am beautiful. Today I will breathe in through my nose and out through my mouth. I will breathe in peace and exhale stress. When I feel myself getting stressed, I will remember to breathe--slowly--calmly.

Thought for the Day:

I breathe in peace and let go of stress.

I Am Beautiful

March 17

I am beautiful. Today I will take time for myself, doing something that makes my blood flow; walking, tai chi, stretching, etc... I will do something that makes my spirit feel free.

Thought for the Day:

I take good care of all of me.

I Am Beautiful

March 18

I am beautiful. Today I will take some time to stretch my neck. I will put my chin to my chest slowly and hold it. I will gently, slowly and carefully tilt my head to the left and right trying to touch my ear to my shoulder. The whole time breathing slowly, in through my nose and out through my mouth.

If I feel myself getting stressed about something, I will pay attention to where I hold it in my body. I will pay attention to the place and gently release it to the Universe.

Thought for the Day:

I am conscious of where I hold my stress.

I Am Beautiful

March 19

I am beautiful. Today I will stretch some more. I will bend over slowly at the hips and stretch out my legs. I will remember to breathe while doing this. I will get outside to walk and listen to the birds.

Thought for the Day:

I am positive in my thoughts, words and actions.

I Am Beautiful

March 20

I am beautiful. Today I will make sure I put nourishing foods into my body. I will eat some protein for every meal. I will drink plenty of water. I will put fresh fruit in my body.

Thought for the Day:

I am mindful to eat well so I may be well in body.

I Am Beautiful

March 21

I am beautiful. Today I will make a list of 5 things I am grateful for. I will remember that to be alive is a gift.

If I catch myself having negative, complaining thoughts, I will stop. I will change my thinking to being appreciative of what I have.

Thought for the Day:

I am thankful for all I have and all I am.

I Am Beautiful

March 22

I am beautiful. Today I will take time to sit still, close my eyes and just breathe. I will let thoughts come and go without judging. I will breathe in peace and breathe out stress.

During the day I will walk slowly with relaxed shoulders.

Thought for the Day:

I am beautiful, loving and peaceful.

March 23

I am beautiful. Today I will focus on behaving with integrity. I will have good intentions with my thoughts, words and actions.

"Integrity is an ongoing process which requires our ongoing attention." --unknown

Thought for the Day:

I say what I mean and mean what I say.

I Am Beautiful

March 24

I am beautiful. Today I will focus my thoughts on what I want in my life. I will think of abundance instead of lack. I will think as if I already have what I want. – Deepak Chopra

Focusing on what I want looks like this: I have loyal friends. I have a peaceful heart. I am healthy. I am compassionate. I have all the money I need.

Thought for the Day:

I am happy and peaceful.

I Am Beautiful

March 25

I am beautiful. Today I will exercise my mind, body and spirit. I will eat well for my body and learn something new for my mind. For my spirit, I will do something that makes me feel free; maybe listen to music or read a book.

Thought for the Day:

I treat myself with gentle patience and respect.

I Am Beautiful

March 26

I am beautiful. Today I will spend some time outside. I will appreciate the beauty of the natural world. I will listen for nature's sounds to fill my heart as I breathe calmly.

Thought for the Day:

I see beauty in everything.

March 27

I am beautiful. I will look for color in the world today. I will look around to see the lovely flowers emerging from their winter sleep. I will look for flowers, budding trees and water.

Thought for the Day:

I breathe in beautiful colors and breathe out stress and judgment.

I Am Beautiful

March 28

I am beautiful. I will take a moment and sit in the grass, put my hands in it and clear my mind of worries and just breathe.

Thought for the Day:

I can handle anything that comes my way.

I Am Beautiful

March 29

I am beautiful. Today I will make a list of beliefs I have; such as, "I believe that males are selfish jerks", "I will never do better in school/work", "I am the ugliest person in my neighborhood" or "I'm clumsy". Then make a list of what you would like it be. For example, "Boys/Men are gentle, kind and giving", "I am successful in whatever I do", "I am beautiful" or "I am coordinated."

When I hear myself think one of these negative beliefs, I will change it to the positive belief I want.

Thought for the Day:

I believe my life to be the way I want.

I Am Beautiful

March 30

I am beautiful. I have wonderful, loving people in my life. Today I will let them know I feel that way.

Thought for the Day:

I show kindness to others.

I Am Beautiful

March 31

I am beautiful. I have beautiful things in my life. Today I will look around me and be grateful for what I have.

Thought for the Day:

I am grateful to be alive.

April

April 1

I am beautiful. Today is a new day, new month. I will start fresh with some stretching and a brisk walk. I will live today as if it's the only day there is; no past and no future.

Thought for the Day:

I love who I am right now.

I Am Beautiful

April 2

I am beautiful. I am a wonderful person with many talents. I will look and listen for reasons why I am here. It may not be what my mind thinks. I might be here to be a smiling face in my neighborhood or a helper for those around me.

Thought for the Day:

I am important.

I Am Beautiful

April 3

I am beautiful. I have people in my life who care about me just for being me. I have people who appreciate my talents and gifts and support me in using them.

Thought for the Day:

I am loving and supportive of myself and others.

April 4

I am beautiful. I will trust myself today. I will listen for my inner voice. I can trust what is right for me.

Thought for the Day:

I believe in myself.

I Am Beautiful

April 5

I am beautiful. I am worthy of good things in my life. I take good care of my physical, mental, emotional and spiritual Selves.

Thought for the Day:

I like who I am and cherish myself.

I Am Beautiful

April 6

I am beautiful. Today is a good day to hold my head up high and be proud of my thoughts, words and actions.

Thought for the Day:

I behave with integrity.

I Am Beautiful

April 7

I am beautiful. Really I am. And so are the flowers that are in bloom right now. I will take the time today to appreciate the beauty of the natural world.

Thought for the Day:

I am happy to be alive.

I Am Beautiful

April 8

I am beautiful. It's a good day to be alive. I will do at least one good deed for someone else today. I will think about someone beside myself.

Thought for the Day:

I am kind and helpful to my fellow wo/man.

I Am Beautiful

April 9

I am beautiful. I am grateful for changes in the weather, because it helps me remember I am constantly changing. When it rains, it reminds me that tears help bring my growth. When the winds blow, it reminds me that new things blow in all the time.

Thought for the Day:

I am beautiful as I grow and change.

I Am Beautiful

April 10

I am beautiful. Today I will look at myself and see what gifts I have been given. I will be grateful for my eyesight, my taste and my legs that get me around. I will be thankful for my hands and my sense of touch.

Thought for the Day:

I see the abundance I have in this moment.

I Am Beautiful

April 11

I am beautiful. I allow myself to be human and make mistakes. I learn from them and make new choices for my highest good.

Thought for the Day:

I am gentle with myself as I learn.

I Am Beautiful

April 12

I am beautiful. There is only one me in this world. I am a unique person and proud of who I am.

"What makes me different, makes me beautiful."- unknown

Thought for the Day:

I see beauty in my uniqueness.

I Am Beautiful

April 13

I am beautiful. Today I will look at the trees and notice which ones are turning green. I will look at the flowers and notice which ones are coming up through the ground and flowering. I will notice how different they are from each other, yet each one is needed to make beauty of the whole.

Thought for the Day:

I am part of world's beauty.

I Am Beautiful

April 14

I am beautiful. I will listen to my gut today. I will pay attention to that voice inside me that leads me in the right direction. I will treat myself with respect and listen to those whispers.

Thought for the Day:

I listen to my gut feelings.

I Am Beautiful

April 15

I am beautiful. When things feel difficult, I will remember to go within. I will ask for help, and then wait for the answer. When I send a prayer into the Universe, I need to remember it is always answered. It may not be what I want, yet it is always answered.

Thought for the Day:

I am patient and kind.

I Am Beautiful

April 16

I am beautiful. I am grateful for the food I have to eat today. I am thankful for being alive. I will take a little time to write down 5 things for which I'm grateful.

Thought for the Day:

I am grateful for my life.

I Am Beautiful

April 17

I am beautiful. I will pay attention today to the thoughts I think. I will change any negative, "putting myself down" thoughts, to ones that lift me up. I will focus on this and write a reminder somewhere I look often.

Thought for the Day:

I give myself love and respect.

I Am Beautiful

April 18

I am beautiful. Day 2 of paying attention to my thoughts. I will really focus today on positive, uplifting thoughts. For example: "I am intelligent and full of great ideas"

Thought for the Day:

I am strong and happy.

I Am Beautiful

April 19

I am beautiful. I am kind, loving and generous. I have good friends around me that support me. I allow myself to let people love me.

When I feel myself resisting receiving, I will stop myself. I will remember to be open to all the goodness available to me from the Universe.

Thought for the Day:

I love myself and allow others to love me too.

I Am Beautiful

April 20

I am beautiful. How hard was it yesterday to think wonderful thoughts about yourself? Was it easy? Today, try it again but with one new thought. Make it a thought about something you want in your life. Say it as if you already have it.

Thought for the Day:

My life is full of health and abundance. (make up your own)

I Am Beautiful

April 21

I am beautiful. I have plenty of money to do the things I want. I have lots of love. I allow people to love me and to give to me. Are these true statements for you? Would you like them to be? The Universe is full of plenty for everyone, including you. Accept it freely, knowing there is more than enough for us all.

Thought for the Day:

I am open to the abundance of the Universe.

I Am Beautiful

April 22

I am beautiful. I am creative in my own way. I was made unique and wonderful. I am an incredible person with special talents and skills.

Thought for the Day:

I see beauty in myself and others.

I Am Beautiful

April 23

I am beautiful. Have you ever noticed how many incredible scents there are in the natural world? Focus today on your breath. Breathe in through your nose and out through your mouth. What new smells do you notice? Do this everywhere you go.

Thought for the Day:

I smell beauty in the world.

I Am Beautiful

April 24

I am beautiful. Today is a great day to smell different flowers that are blooming. I will pay attention and sniff all I can, even ones I don't think have a fragrance. Wow! I never knew!

If I walk by one and forget to lean down and smell it, I will be gentle with myself and remember to smell the next one.

Thought for the Day:

I am beautiful and unique like every flower.

I Am Beautiful

April 25

I am beautiful. I learn -- that stretches my mind. I exercise -- that stretches my body. I pray -- that stretches my soul. I create -- that stretches my spirit. I am a complete person.

If I feel I am lacking in any of these areas, I will take a look at myself and see what I could do differently. I will take time to find more balance.

Thought for the Day:

I make gentle observations and tiny corrections.

I Am Beautiful

April 26

I am beautiful. I will take what I observed yesterday about myself and gently make a small change. I will add something or take something away. I will see myself as a wonderful person no matter what.

Thought for the Day:

I love me in my process.

I Am Beautiful

April 27

I am beautiful. I love and cherish who I am. I take good care of all aspects of my being. I am willing to change.

Thought for the Day:

I think kind thoughts and eat healthy foods.

I Am Beautiful

April 28

I am beautiful. I will walk today with my head held high. I will think positive thoughts all day long. If someone says or does something which irritates me to the point of being negative, I will send them love and gently bring myself back to the positive.

Thought for the Day:

I am happy, healthy and love who I am.

I Am Beautiful

April 29

I am beautiful. Today I will feel; I will notice my moods, not judge myself, just notice. I will try to see myself as if I'm the person sitting next to me.

Thought for the Day:

I am becoming a better me.

I Am Beautiful

April 30

I am beautiful. What is the weather like today? Is the sun shining? Is it raining? You have no control over the weather; just like you have no control over anyone else or their actions. You do have control over yourself and how you react. If it's raining, get out an umbrella and be cheerful. If someone is being unpleasant, don't be around them.

Thought for the Day:

I make choices best for me.

May

May 1

I am beautiful. Today is a new day. I will take time to see beauty in at least two things I thought were ugly. I will look in the mirror and find at least two things about myself that are beautiful, too.

Thought for the Day:

I see beauty in all things.

May 2

I am beautiful. Life is so interesting. New beginnings, new endings, transitions – May is such a transition month. Winter has ended yet tries to keep its fingers grasping the world. Spring has begun, trying to get a grip on things. It's not quite warm all the time and not quite cold all the time either. It's transition time. Transitions can be somewhat difficult. Not knowing what to expect, there can be a sense of being out of control.

Thought for the Day:

I am at peace. Everything is how it needs to be.

I Am Beautiful

May 3

I am beautiful. It's amazing to me how everything happens in its own time. There are flowers that have bloomed and gone, and others that are just blooming now. Some trees are a beautiful, spring green while others are still leafless. This helps me realize that I will bloom in my own time. I am beautiful here and now where I stand. I don't have to change anything but how I see myself.

Thought for the Day:

I am content in this moment.

I Am Beautiful

May 4

I am beautiful. Today is a good day to show someone you care about them. It's the little things that make people smile. Try surprising someone with a phone call or a note. Let them know it's you or make it anonymous.

Thought for the Day:

I do nice things for people without expecting anything in return.

I Am Beautiful

May 5

I am beautiful. Today I am going to put my focus on people I love, and things I love to do. If I start to focus on things and people who make my life miserable, I will stop. I will acknowledge that those things and people are there, and then turn back to things that make me feel grateful for my life.

Thought for the Day:

I am happy to be alive and sharing my gifts with others.

I Am Beautiful

May 6

I am beautiful. Today I will remember one thing I am working on changing. I will think good thoughts about myself, and be patient and gentle.

Thought for the Day:

I believe in myself and trust I am taken care of always.

I Am Beautiful

May 7

I am beautiful. I believe that every day is a fabulous day regardless of the weather; every day that I have a body to walk, talk, see, smell and hear, is a beautiful day. I am grateful for what I have.

Thought for the Day:

I see the beauty in myself.

May 8

I am beautiful. NOW IS LATER. When I think that I'll do something later, later is really just another time's now. Now is a previous time's later. So Now is the only time there ever is to feel beautiful.

Thought for the Day:

I see each moment as the only moment.

I Am Beautiful

May 9

I am beautiful. Today I'm feeling kind of icky. I'm acknowledging how I feel and letting myself just be in it. I will not judge it and will be gentle with myself. It is a good time to be grateful for days I feel well.

Thought for the Day:

I have an abundance of happiness and health.

I Am Beautiful

May 10

I am beautiful. Today I want to attract peace and love into the many parts of my day. I will do this by focusing on peaceful and loving thoughts.

Thought for the Day:

I allow myself and others to be who they are.

I Am Beautiful

May 11

I am beautiful. While on my morning walk, I overheard a runner saying to his running mate, "I owe it to myself to be the best that I can be." It seems to me that if we all had such an attitude, this world would be a different place.

Thought for the Day:

Whoever I am... I want to be the best of that!

I Am Beautiful

May 12

I am beautiful. I start my day today with a heart full of joy and thanksgiving. I am happy to be alive another day.

Thought for the Day:

I am full of joy.

I Am Beautiful

May 13

I am beautiful. Today is a great day to create what I want for my future - to pay attention to my thoughts and deliberately create what I want. It is a great day to allow others to be who they are without the negativity of just tolerating them.

Thought for the Day:

Sunshine emanates from my heart.

I Am Beautiful

May 14

I am beautiful. The changing of the seasons is such a beautiful thing. The nights get warmer along with the days. The windows open, the house gets aired out. The scent of flowers wafts through the house. What a joy it is to have a changing of the seasons.

Thought for the Day:

I breathe in change, I breathe out acceptance.

I Am Beautiful

May 15

I am beautiful. Rain is one of the most amazing things. It gives our plants the liquid they need to survive. It freshens up the world. It rejuvenates. A rainy day is truly a blessing.

Thought for the Day:

Rain, like tears, refreshes me.

I Am Beautiful

May 16

I am beautiful. Today is a new day with wonderful new things coming my way. Since I create with my thoughts, I know what is coming. I don't know <u>how</u> it's coming, yet I know that if I pay attention to my thoughts and focus on what I want with great emotion and great expectation (Abraham-Hicks), I will receive it.

Thought for the Day:

I am grateful for all I have and all I am.

I Am Beautiful

May 17

I am beautiful. Today I commit to finish a goal; finish something I have had on my mind. It could be writing a letter to a friend I've been thinking about, start a book I've been telling myself I would write. I will start with today and on purpose begin to finish one of my goals.

Thought for the Day:

I let go of guilt and choose to love myself.

I Am Beautiful

May 18

I am beautiful. I am so grateful to have three healthy children. I am also grateful to work with those who are different – those born without their hearing and with body abnormalities. It has not only stretched my own compassion, but has also changed my perspective on what I find important in life.

Thought for the Day:

I see beauty in all people and beings.

I Am Beautiful

May 19

I am beautiful. It's amazing, when you think you have it all figured out, life throws you a curve ball. It then sits back and watches what you do with it. Will you duck and pretend you didn't see it? Or will you swing and give it all you've got?

Thought for the Day:

I can handle whatever comes my way.

I Am Beautiful

May 20

I am beautiful. Sometimes it is difficult to know what the right thing to do is. That's when I follow my heart and ask for help. If I listen to my head, it confuses me. My heart is never wrong. Doing the right thing isn't always the most popular thing. In the long run, you'll find out that it was all worth it.

Thought for the Day:

My heart guides me to do the right thing.

I Am Beautiful

May 21

I am beautiful. It is a great day to organize some things. Those things could be physical, or they could be mental. Cleaning house physically may not be an issue, but cleaning house mentally, emotionally or spiritually might be. Today is a great day to look at those things that I need to put back in order.

Thought for the Day:

I am organized, clear and happy.

I Am Beautiful

May 22

I am beautiful. Every day is such a gift. It is important to look at life in this way. If you can open yourself to the beauty in every moment around you, you can open yourself to the beauty within yourself.

Thought for the Day:

I trust and love myself every moment of this day.

I Am Beautiful

May 23

I am beautiful. Today is a super day to be grateful for things that help me grow; Intellectual challenges (mental), emotional challenges (things that stretch my heart), spiritual challenges (things/experiences that help me remember to ask for help) and physical challenges.

Thought for the Day:

I am surrounded by Love.

I Am Beautiful

May 24

I am beautiful. This is such a beautiful day. The clouds have varying degrees of purple and blues. As I remember to breathe in through my nose and out through my mouth, I get calmer on the inside. I remember to slow down and be grateful for all I have and all I am.

Thought for the Day:

I am happy, healthy, grounded, safe and free.

I Am Beautiful

May 25

I am beautiful. I take good care of myself. I eat well. I exercise my body. I pay attention to my thoughts. I have fun, and give myself time to relax. It is a great day to check my balance and tweak areas where I am out of balance.

Thought for the Day:

I live in balance.

I Am Beautiful

May 26

I am beautiful. It makes me feel good to do things for other people, to take care of their needs. When I put a smile on someone's face, I put a smile in my heart. I can't help but feel beautiful on the outside when I feel happy on the inside.

Thought for the Day:

I carry kindness and peace wherever I go.

I Am Beautiful

May 27

I am beautiful. Sometimes things happen over which you have no control. Let them go. Remember what you do have control of; yourself, your thoughts, your actions.

Thought for the Day:

I have control of my thoughts.

I Am Beautiful

May 28

I am beautiful. I am so grateful to have another day with my loved ones. Taking the time to be in the moment with them helps me feel good about myself.

Thought for the Day:

I share the Light within me with those around me.

I Am Beautiful

May 29

I am beautiful. In a moment of frustration I blurted out, "I don't care!" But realizing what I said, corrected it and said, *"That's not true. I do care. I care deeply. That's why I'm so frustrated."* I not only caught myself, but changed it immediately. This allowed me to not feel guilty for any length of time. I've learned that guilt doesn't serve the world in any way, so not to give it any energy.

Thought for the Day:

I give energy to positive thoughts such as, I am precious and wonderful.

I Am Beautiful

May 30

I am beautiful. After talking to two of my friends this morning in the coffee shop before work, I was reminded of a couple things. One, it is important what we put in our bodies physically. Two, it is important what we put in our bodies mentally – our thoughts. Thoughts create, as does the food that makes up our cells. As people on this planet, we have a right and a responsibility to be aware – to think – to create our lives the way we want them.

Thought for the Day:

I create my day with thoughts I think and choices I make.

I Am Beautiful

May 31

I am beautiful. There is hardly anything more special than a child's smile or giggle. It makes me happy when I look in the mirror to see the child that's inside me, smile back.

Thought for the Day:

I walk with beauty. I am beauty. I give beauty.

June

June 1

I am beautiful. I am very careful with whom I choose to be around. I choose my friends with great care; just like I choose my thoughts with great care. My thoughts influence my physical world. My friends influence my choices.

Thought for the Day:

I make good choices for me.

I Am Beautiful

June 2

I am beautiful. I was reminded today to be grateful for all I have. There will always be someone who has more and always someone who has less than I. I was reminded to make my corner of the world the best place it can be.

Thought for the Day:

I see beauty in my life.

I Am Beautiful

June 3

I am beautiful. Each and every moment is such a miracle. If you look for beauty in the world, you will find it. Today I left my house with a certain grumpiness about me. I visited some friends, knit for about three hours, and returned home with a completely different mood. This helped me realize how important it is to take care of myself.

Thought for the Day:

I nurture myself.

I Am Beautiful

June 4

I am beautiful. The sweet scent of the end of spring and beginning of summer. Trees and bushes have bloomed and given off their fragrance. They are so willing to share without judgment of who they are giving to, or wondering what they will get in return. They give their best and most beautiful without regard to whether anyone is looking. What would the world be like if people were the same? What would each individual be like if they gave the best and most beautiful part of themselves each and every moment?

Thought for the Day:

I am as beautiful as a flower in bloom.

I Am Beautiful

June 5

I am beautiful. I take this day to do my best, even though I'm not feeling very well. I'm feeling congested, fatigued and blue. Yet what I choose to think will be different than how I feel.

Thought for the Day:

I am energetic, loving and happy.

I Am Beautiful

June 6

I am beautiful. I hand my worries over to my angels. They have asked me to have a better balance of heaven and earth. They say that my supply is truly limitless and that I need to work hand-in-hand with the Divine. How do I know this? I keep seeing the numbers 644, like $6.44 or 6:44. I look in my reference book written by Dr. Doreen Virtue, <u>Healing with the Angels</u>. It has many combinations of numbers that the angels use to communicate with us. This is an important tool I use often for myself.

Thought for the Day:

I hand my worries to my angels.

I Am Beautiful

June 7

I am beautiful. This morning, while waiting for the weather report before work, I saw a little blurb on TV about secrets. One of the secrets was there is someone who cannot look in the mirror because they feel ugly. What a tragedy. Everyone is beautiful in their own way. Everyone is beautiful; they need to believe.

Thought for the Day:

I see beauty inside and outside myself.

I Am Beautiful

June 8

I am beautiful. I am so grateful for all I have and all I am. When I see someone working their tail off, I am filled with a sense of pride. I am proud of them for working hard to better their situation.

Thought for the Day:

I am a strong, beautiful person.

I Am Beautiful

June 9

I am beautiful. I get reminded every day at work about the little things that are so important in our daily lives.

"Big hug please," she murmured in speech that only someone who spends a lot of time with her could understand.

"Big hug please," I repeated for the woman trying to guess what she was saying.

"You made my day!" the lunch lady exclaimed with an endearing look on her face.

It's moments like these that show me how precious life is, especially the little things.

Thought for the Day:

My life is full of precious moments.

I Am Beautiful

June 10

I am beautiful. It rained last night. The air feels so fresh and cool. I feel so fresh and beautiful too. I breathe in the cool, clean air and breathe out all ugliness I feel. I fill my heart with good feelings. I fill my head with good thoughts. I fill my soul with peaceful joy of another day.

Thought for the Day:

I have loving, gentle thoughts.

I Am Beautiful

June 11

I am beautiful. What a great day to be alive. This is yesterday's tomorrow. Did I attract what I wanted through my thoughts? If not, today is another day to work on it. I need to remember that I attract what is in my life through my thoughts.

Thought for the Day:

I am happy, healthy, well-rested, safe, prosperous and free.

I Am Beautiful

June 12

I am beautiful. Today on my morning walk, I saw four deer. They looked young and beautiful; three females and one male. I came home and read about deer in my book <u>Animal Speak</u> by Ted Andrews. I then read about the significance of number four in my book <u>Healing with the Angels</u> by Dr. Doreen Virtue.

Thought for the Day:

I cultivate gentleness and beauty in myself.

I Am Beautiful

June 13

I am beautiful. The sky is blue, birds are singing, trees have beautiful leaves; another day with a purpose to fulfill. This world is a beautiful place if I choose to see it that way.

Thought for the Day:

I am happy and healthy.

I Am Beautiful

June 14

I am beautiful. What else can I say? I look in the mirror and see the spark in my eyes that says, "I am part of all that exists." When you look in the mirror do you see the beauty that is you? Do you look in your eyes and see your beautiful light?

Thought for the Day:

I love who I am.

I Am Beautiful

June 15

I am beautiful. What a fabulous day to be grateful for all I have. I am so happy to have my eyesight to see, my legs to walk, my ears to hear. The world holds such beauty for us all.

Thought for the Day:

I am open to my own beauty.

I Am Beautiful

June 16

I am beautiful. It is raining this morning. The rain gives me a special feeling. It cleanses the world, makes it smell better and gives the plants water to drink. Rain is amazing. Without it, we would not be alive.

Thought for the Day:

The rain washes me beautiful.

June 17

I am beautiful. I am guided, protected and loved. I will make loving choices for myself today; in what I think, say and do.

Thought for the Day:

I am a blessing.

I Am Beautiful

June 18

I am beautiful. Today is the anniversary of my birth. I am so happy to be alive. This day has been all about me and I deserve all of it. I can't remember any year feeling as good as this one. I finally appreciate who I am and who I am becoming. I finally love myself and can share that with the people around me.

Thought for the Day:

I am happy to be me.

I Am Beautiful

June 19

I am beautiful. I pulled up my car, parked and opened my door. Wow! An incredible fragrance came over me. It was so attractive that I immediately stepped out of the car and pulled a bunch of leaves and feathery flowers to my nose. The fragrance reminded me of the beauty everywhere I go. Nothing has to be done to these trees to be beautiful. Therefore, nothing has to be done to us to make us beautiful.

Thought for the Day:

I open my heart to the beauty within me and outside me.

I Am Beautiful

June 20

I am beautiful. What a great day to pay attention to your thoughts! "Your thoughts attract like a magnet." - Abraham-Hicks. Are you attracting what you want? If you think you are beautiful and feel you are beautiful, then you are beautiful – you emanate beauty.

Thought for the Day:

I have great beauty. I have great joy.

I Am Beautiful

June 21

I am beautiful. Everyone born is unique and has a right to be here. We are all beautiful, magnificent, beloved children of Life.

Thought for the Day:

I am equally as special as anyone else.

I Am Beautiful

June 22

I am beautiful. Today is beautiful. I'm happy to have another day to be here and share with people in my life. The nice thing about my friends is they don't need me to talk with them all the time. They know I'm here when they need me and vice versa.

Thought for the Day:

I am blessed with my relationships.

I Am Beautiful

June 23

I am beautiful. What a lovely day it is. The sky is blue, the sun is shining and the Linden trees are in bloom. Their fragrance is indescribable. On my morning walk in the cemetery, there was a swallow not wanting me to come in to the grounds. It kept flying in circles, making a raucous and diving straight for my head. After looking up "swallow" in my book <u>Animal Speak</u> by Ted Andrews, I learned that I am in need of making sure my teenagers are being protected from themselves. I need to keep making my home a warm and safe place to be.

Thought for the Day:

I learn, love, laugh and keep my children safe. (Even if it's just my inner child)

I Am Beautiful

June 24

I am beautiful. I am incredibly lucky! Why? Because I have another day to be the best I can; the best in making positive changes for myself. This is another day to practice those things that I am doing to change my life.

Thought for the Day:

I am prosperous and loving.

I Am Beautiful

June 25

I am beautiful. A warm wind is blowing today. I wonder what incredible thing it will blow in for me. Our thoughts are ever-changing like the wind. If we can harness our thoughts, we can change the world. Our thoughts are that powerful.

Thought for the Day:

I am loving, happy, prosperous and free.

I Am Beautiful

June 26

I am beautiful. Even though change is happening all around me, I maintain my center – I maintain my inner beauty – my peace – my love for myself. I know that unless I take care of myself I cannot take care of other things.

Thought for the Day:

I honor my change.

I Am Beautiful

June 27

I am beautiful. I live. There is no mistake about it, I live. I don't spend my time cleaning everything in my life. I clean to keep things sanitary – but spotless – no way. Getting dirty and having dirt is a reality of life. Without it there would be no food. I am grateful to be alive.

Thought for the Day:

I take good care of myself and surroundings.

I Am Beautiful

June 28

I am beautiful. The funny thing about our lives is that beliefs are a matter of mind. All of us have different beliefs. Our beliefs are ours only. There may be other people with similar ones. But in the end our beliefs are as individual as snowflakes.

Thought for the Day:

I have a calm and beautiful mind.

I Am Beautiful

June 29

I am beautiful. Today is a cloudy, cold day – perfect for introspection. It's a great day to get grounded and take care of myself. I will take note of my inner beauty, strengths and my weaknesses.

Thought for the Day:

I accept me as I am - weaknesses and all.

I Am Beautiful

June 30

I am beautiful. I love when I have lots of energy. It feels so good. So I choose to eat foods that make me feel energized. Today I will pay attention to everything I put in my body; how it makes me feel and how long its energy lasts.

Thought for the Day:

I feed my body foods that give me long-lasting energy.

July

July 1

I am beautiful. A new month, a new day, a new commitment to myself - Who am I? What do I do to improve the world? I commit to knowing myself, loving myself, and loving others.

Thought for the Day:

I am kind and loving.

I Am Beautiful

July 2

I am beautiful. Today on my walk I saw a mama deer with her two babies. I was walking later than I usually do - what a beautiful sight that was for me. Watching her take her young to a safe place was a reminder to me that I need to make sure my young are in a safe place. Am I safe emotionally for them? Am I safe physically? Am I safe spiritually?

Thought for the Day:

I am loving, gentle and safe for all around me.

I Am Beautiful

July 3

I am beautiful. What an incredible day. The birds are chirping, the sky is crystal clear blue and the trees are flowering. I am so happy to be alive. To quote Forrest Gump, "Life is like a box of chocolates, you never know what you're gonna get."

Thought for the Day:

I am clear and strong.

I Am Beautiful

July 4

I am beautiful. I celebrate my independence today – my independence from others' views, others' beliefs of who I am, others' thoughts of what beauty is. I celebrate my own life today. I will do what it is that makes me happy and feel beautiful.

Thought for the Day:

I am who I am who I am.

I Am Beautiful

July 5

I am beautiful. It's important for me to recognize when I'm feeling blue. It's also important to realize it's a passing state. If I don't acknowledge it though, it lingers. Feelings for me are like clouds. They come and cover the sun for a little bit and then pass on through. I am grateful for the cloudy times, for they make me appreciate my sunny times.

Thought for the Day:

I acknowledge my feelings, good or bad.

I Am Beautiful

July 6

I am beautiful. When I wake up feeling bad, it gives me the opportunity to be thankful for those days I wake up feeling good.

Thought for the Day:

I am healthy and feel good.

I Am Beautiful

July 7

I am beautiful. I will not let anyone tell me otherwise. I will see and feel the beauty in myself. If someone tries to tell me otherwise, I will not participate in their darkness.

Thought for the Day:

I am as beautiful as the sun.

I Am Beautiful

July 8

I am beautiful. This is such a lovely day. It's raining; a gentle, quiet, soaking rain. The sky is gray, yet bright with light. I am so grateful to have this day to continue growing.

Thought for the Day:

I grow with grace and ease.

I Am Beautiful

July 9

I am beautiful. I am grateful for the animals in my life. They are always here for me. Regardless of my mood, they love me anyway. Especially when I'm feeling sad, they are here for me.

Thought for the Day:

I am loved, loving and loveable.

I Am Beautiful

July 10

I am beautiful. So is the world around me. There were many Robins out today. This let me know that my new growth is spreading, and not just in one area. It reminded me that balance of life is very delicate. My life, the birds' lives, everyone's life is such a gift.

Thought for the Day:

I am connected with everything. What I do to another, I do to myself.

I Am Beautiful

July 11

I am beautiful. As I get older, I also get wiser and more beautiful. I will look in the mirror, at my eyes, and say three things I like about myself.

Thought for the Day:

I love myself. I see beauty inside me. I am loveable.

I Am Beautiful

July 12

I am beautiful. Dreams are interesting. I often write them down to read later. Doing this allows me to understand more of what they were trying to tell me.

Thought for the Day:

I am happy and healthy.

I Am Beautiful

July 13

I am beautiful. Today I am going to work on changing one belief. I will make a list of 5 beliefs, such as "I believe that males are selfish jerks", or "I will never do better in school/work" or "I am the ugliest person in my neighborhood".

When I hear myself think one of these beliefs, I will turn it around. For example, "Boys/Men are kind and giving" or "I am successful in whatever I do".

Thought for the Day:

I am beautiful inside and out always.

I Am Beautiful

July 14

I am beautiful. I am lucky to have another day to be alive; to watch the world change, to watch those around me change, to watch myself change. Change is the only thing that never changes.

Thought for the Day:

I accept change as it comes. I always see myself as beautiful.

I Am Beautiful

July 15

I am beautiful. What a great day to pay attention to my thoughts and practice loving myself. I'll look for what motivates my thoughts and actions. Is it fear or is it love? It's a great day to practice love.

Thought for the Day:

I love who I am. I love who I am. I love who I am.

I Am Beautiful

July 16

I am beautiful. I am grateful for this day. Today I will still pay attention to my thoughts and change them when they are negative. I will be patient with myself when I notice a thought I don't want. I will turn it around to what I want it to be.

Thought for the Day:

I am kind and gentle with myself.

I Am Beautiful

July 17

I am beautiful. And so are summer flowers, trees and weather; to walk outside in shorts and a t-shirt; to feel the summer warmth on my skin. I am so grateful I can feel, smell, hear and see.

Thought for the Day:

I show my beauty with my actions.

I Am Beautiful

July 18

I am beautiful. I am beautiful. I am beautiful. Need I say more?

Thought for the Day:

I am truly beautiful.

I Am Beautiful

July 19

I am beautiful. Another day to practice positive thinking; I am so proud of myself and my progress. (Yes, I am. Ignore the voice that says you're not.) I keep in mind that I am OK just the way I am, as I work to advance myself to higher thinking and being.

Thought for the Day:

I see everything in the world as beautiful, even when it's not pretty.

I Am Beautiful

July 20

I am beautiful. I can do this. I can do this. I can do this. Whatever it is that challenges me today, I can do. I believe in myself and take good care of myself with loving thoughts.

Thought for the Day:

I love, encourage, and support myself in my goals.

I Am Beautiful

July 21

I am beautiful. When the days of summer are so hot, I wake up early and enjoy the cool air. It gives me time to reflect, see animals awake that time of day, and see the beauty of sunrises.

Thought for the Day:

I cherish every moment.

I Am Beautiful

July 22

I am beautiful. Today I saw a fox on my walk. It was beautiful in its foxness. It was so swift, silent, alert, and then it was gone. I think it was telling me to be still and silent in my loveliness.

Thought for the Day:

I am beautiful in my humanness.

I Am Beautiful

July 23

I am beautiful. Getting together with friends is a delicate balancing act for me. I enjoy their company and also enjoy being alone. I have to be careful and make sure I maintain harmony within myself.

Thought for the Day:

I am harmonious and beautiful.

I Am Beautiful

July 24

I am beautiful. How many times do we talk about things we know to do, yet don't do them? For example, "Exercise makes me feel so good" or "Eating vegetables helps me think more clearly." Today I will pay attention to what I say and actually do those things.

Thought for the Day:

I walk my talk.

I Am Beautiful

July 25

I am beautiful. It's easy for me to look at someone else and pick out things I don't like about them. It's much harder to realize that what I see in them is also inside me. Today I will practice noticing myself in others when I pick out their negative qualities.

Thought for the Day:

I see myself in others.

I Am Beautiful

July 26

I am beautiful. It's important to have goals. It's much easier to reach those goals when you have "clarity of intent". –Don Miguel Ruiz, The Four Agreements

Thought for the Day:

My intentions have power.

I Am Beautiful

July 27

I am beautiful. It's easier being harsh with myself than it is being nice to myself. Why is this? Today I will pay extra attention to noticing my negative self-talk and changing it to positive self-talk, especially in the little things.

Thought for the Day:

I see, speak and feel beauty inside me.

I Am Beautiful

July 28

I am beautiful. Every day when I wake, I have to remind myself that I'm here for a reason, I'm a beautiful person, and I'm thankful for another day. This is all before I step out of bed.

Thought for the Day:

I awake to the beauty that is me.

I Am Beautiful

July 29

I am beautiful. Today I will pay attention to my senses. I will feel and hear my breath as air flows in and out of my lungs. I will smell and taste the air around me. I will see beauty around me, and see beauty in me.

Thought for the Day:

I breathe in beauty and breathe out negative thoughts.

I Am Beautiful

July 30

I am beautiful. Today I will sit and write down a list of everything I want in my life. These aren't just material wishes. They are spiritual, intellectual, emotional, relationships, etc.... Put everything on your list; even things you think are miniscule – like a pretty bowl to put my jewelry in before I shower. Know as you make this list, the world has no boundaries- it's limitless.

Thought for the Day:

I can have it all.

I Am Beautiful

July 31

I am beautiful. Today I will think about one obstacle keeping me from having something from yesterday's list. I will focus on the opposite thought of the obstacle. e.g. "I don't have enough money." Change it to, "I have plenty of money."

Thought for the Day:

I deserve good things and good people.

August

August 1

I am beautiful. I take this first day of a new month to reassess my focus. I choose peace in my heart. As I go through my day, if I start to feel restless, I will close my eyes and remember I am as peaceful and beautiful as a sleeping baby.

Thought for the Day:

I breathe in peace and breathe out beauty.

I Am Beautiful

August 2

I am beautiful. As I think about the balance of the Universe, I know I have light and dark qualities, too. Today I will name three dark/negative qualities in me and then see the opposite light/positive ones too. I can be a whole balanced person if I acknowledge my dark traits of being human.

Thought for the Day:

I embrace my negative while focusing on my positive.

I Am Beautiful

August 3

I am beautiful. The longer I live, the more I learn coincidences have meaning and are not just happenstance. "Never ignore a coincidence," says Deepak Chopra. Today I will take note of synchronicities big and small that happen to me.

Thought for the Day:

I am a beautiful part of the whole.

I Am Beautiful

August 4

I am beautiful. As I look for more coincidences today, I will pay attention to how the world works together in an amazing dance. – Deepak Chopra

Thought for the Day:

I go with the flow of life.

I Am Beautiful

August 5

I am beautiful. Today is a non-comparison day. It's easy to see someone and say, "I wish my hair was like that" or "I wish I were that skinny". The thing is, you are beautiful just the way you are. So embrace every aspect of you and love yourself.

Thought for the Day:

I am beautiful just as I am.

I Am Beautiful

August 6

I am beautiful. Everything I do today, I will give my best effort. I will set my intention and carry it out in my every action; from pouring tea to saying hello to those around me.

Thought for the Day:

I give my best to everyone and everything.

I Am Beautiful

August 7

I am beautiful. Today I will pay attention to the emotions I attach to my thoughts. As I go through my day, I will add intentional emotion to my thoughts. Say this with emotion and without it: "I am beautiful." Which one feels better?

Thought for the Day:

I am beautiful.

I Am Beautiful

August 8

I am beautiful. After attending a diksha/deeksha this weekend, I learned again that until we heal from past wounds, we cannot move forward. Some of my past wounds have been inflicted by others. Some have been inflicted by myself. When I look in the mirror and say I'm ugly, that's a self-inflicting wound. It's important that we all learn to love ourselves so we can spread that love and energy to others.

Thought for the Day:

I am loved, loving and loveable.

I Am Beautiful

August 9

I am beautiful. Some days, the best thing to do is stay home and take care of you. Today is one of those days for me. You see, yesterday I came down with a sore throat and runny nose. They both got progressively worse throughout the day. I drank green tea all day long and rested. Today, I feel I'm on the way toward healing. I want to continue that, so I took today off work. I realize that to take good care of myself, I need to focus on caring for me.

Thought for the Day:

I am worthy of loving care.

I Am Beautiful

August 10

I am beautiful. Everyone takes care of their house and home the way they want to. Since my body is also my home, I take good care of it. When I start ignoring my body, I become increasingly uncomfortable.

Thought for the Day:

I cherish my body.

I Am Beautiful

August 11

I am beautiful. This is another day of not comparing yourself to others. It's a non-judgment day; not of yourself or others. Look in the mirror, don't judge, just look at the light in your eyes and smile at yourself.

Thought for the Day:

I am beautiful just as I am.

I Am Beautiful

August 12

I am beautiful. There are things in life that are beautiful, yet you wouldn't see it unless you are looking, and digging deep. Like people for one – we are all unique. Inside every one of us is a spark of Light. Some of us may carry a heavy shell of anger/guilt/fear, etc… yet inside is still that spark.

Thought for the Day:

I am light, love and truly beautiful.

I Am Beautiful

August 13

I am beautiful. Little things in life are often the most special and meaningful to me; like a phone call from one of my children or a bird that sits near me on my lunch break. What little things have meaning for you?

Thought for the Day:

I see and love little things about myself.

I Am Beautiful

August 14

I am beautiful. Today I will step out of my comfort zone and say hi to someone I usually wouldn't talk to. I will feel good about doing it and it will probably make them feel good too.

Thought for the Day:

I share myself with others.

I Am Beautiful

August 15

I am beautiful. I am blessed with another day. What a gift! I am grateful for my legs that walk, my eyes that see, my ears that hear. I am grateful for the gifts that I have been given.

Thought for the Day:

I allow myself to love myself.

I Am Beautiful

August 16

I am beautiful. This is a big "gear-up-for-change" time; schools start soon, weather is starting to change and animals are starting to change their routines too. Since change is the theme, today I will work on starting to change one negative belief I have.

Thought for the Day:

I make room for change. I am _____.
(Insert new belief)

I Am Beautiful

August 17

I am beautiful. Little children are so adaptable. There is so much to learn from them; no grudges, no judgment, only love. In the end, love is who we are, where we came from and where we are going.

Thought for the Day:

I am love.

I Am Beautiful

August 18

I am beautiful. We all have our own way of thinking and doing things. I love that about the world. If we can now learn to allow others to think their own way and believe their own beliefs, our world would be a much gentler place.

Thought for the Day:

I allow people to be who they are.

I Am Beautiful

August 19

I am beautiful. We all say or do the wrong thing at times. We're human. Still, we are all OK the way we are, and we were made to learn as we go. It's good to be gentle with ourselves as we make mistakes.

Thought for the Day:

I learn from my mistakes and love myself anyway.

I Am Beautiful

August 20

I am beautiful. Today I picked out orange and dark blue to wear. I love to change up colors on my body. If I'm in need of a mood change, I'll wear bright colors. Colors have many meanings and are important for many reasons.

Thought for the Day:

I am happy in any color.

I Am Beautiful

August 21

I am beautiful. It's important to surround myself with things I find pretty and gentle. What counts is how they make me feel. What other people think is not important. If someone else likes them, it's just a bonus.

Thought for the Day:

I'm surrounded by beauty. I am beauty.

I Am Beautiful

August 22

I am beautiful. It feels good to do something nice for someone else. It could be holding a door as you go in the market, or slowing down to allow a driver with their turn signal on to get in front of you. Even though you may never get a thank you, it still feels good to spread niceness.

Thought for the Day:

I look for ways to help other beings.

I Am Beautiful

August 23

I am beautiful. Autumn is beginning to show itself. Leaves are just barely starting to turn. The temperature difference from morning to night is 40º. What an incredible day to slow down and become aware of your surroundings.

Thought for the Day:

I open my eyes to the beauty within me and without.

I Am Beautiful

August 24

I am beautiful. So is the world. The full-moon was in its orange-yellow splendor the other night. Autumn... it's on its way. This is a great time to reflect on changes needed in your own life. Take your thinking, for example. Are you thinking thoughts that will create your life the way you want it to be?

Thought for the Day:

I am at peace. I open my heart to change.

I Am Beautiful

August 25

I am beautiful. Things I love about my life; a light rain giving the earth a drink, a light breeze blowing wisps of my hair, sun shining on my shoulders, a friend's hug in the morning. What are things you love about your day, your life?

Thought for the Day:

I shine like the sun.

I Am Beautiful

August 26

I am beautiful. It's a great day to take notice of what I would like to change in my life. The trees are starting to change so I will too. I will find a small thing about my life that needs some fine tuning. And I'll start on it today.

Thought for the Day:

I am capable of great change, one small step at a time.

I Am Beautiful

August 27

I am beautiful. Days are getting noticeably shorter and evenings are getting cooler. Some of the trees are starting to turn into their autumn colors a little at a time. The bees are getting more aggressive knowing their time is limited. It's amazing how every day is a gift and our earth time is limited too. I am so grateful for this day. Another one to do my best, be who I am, grow into a better human being.

Thought for the Day:

I embrace change and love who I am in the process.

I Am Beautiful

August 28

I am beautiful. These cooler days in August are so nice for me. As a person who cannot handle the heat, I welcome cooler days of fall. The smells in the autumn air are also distinct from any other season. There is a fragrant pungency I so enjoy. It's different than the newness of spring or maturity of summer. It has the scent of decomposing, drying out and completion. Now is the time where the end of summer draws nearer to the beginning of fall.

Thought for the Day:

I am who I am, and I am grateful for who I'm becoming.

I Am Beautiful

August 29

I am beautiful. Yesterday on my morning walk I came face to face with a mule deer. It was amazing! It was quiet and still. It stood there like a statue. I stood there too respecting the quiet acknowledgement that we both knew the other was there. It was really a special moment in my day.

Thought for the Day:

All creatures are important in this world, including me.

I Am Beautiful

August 30

I am beautiful. I woke up this morning angry; angry at this moment for being the way it is, angry at those in charge for it not being the way I asked, angry at myself for expecting others to make the change for me. I then realized I am the one who needs to make the change. If I don't act to make the change, others will let me keep doing what I've always done. I am important enough to take good care of myself. It's my responsibility to make the change for myself.

Thought for the Day:

I am responsible for me and my own changes.

I Am Beautiful

August 31

I am beautiful. This world is such an amazing place with so much diversity. I want others to appreciate me in my uniqueness, so today, I will look at others in their uniqueness. Instead of looking at others like they are different; different religion, different skin color, different clothes… I will focus on how we are all humans with feelings and stories.

Thought for the Day:

I see those around me as diverse and beautiful.

September

September 1

I am beautiful. So are the gifts we give to each other. Today my teenage daughter chose to spend time with me. Not just an hour, but all-day kind of time. I know it was an effort for her. And I also know she has no idea what a gift it was for me; the gift of her time.

Thought for the Day:

My time is a gift I share. I share freely.

I Am Beautiful

September 2

I am beautiful. We all have a story to tell. We all have a childhood and were adolescents. Our stories, our memories, helped get us to this moment. The thing to remember is where we are is this moment. We are not our past stories.

Thought for the Day:

I am healthy and whole right now.

I Am Beautiful

September 3

I am beautiful. On my Yogi tea bag this morning was this quote, "Life is a flow of love: only your participation is requested."- Yogi Bhajan

I can't think of a better way to say, "love yourself, love all else." You don't have to, although life sure is more enjoyable when you do.

Thought for the Day:

I love who I am right now.

I Am Beautiful

September 4

I am beautiful. I love to be in a peaceful place by myself. It gives me the chance to listen to my inner voice and become centered. If you love yourself, you'll enjoy time with you.

Thought for the Day:

I enjoy my own company.

I Am Beautiful

September 5

I am beautiful. I am grateful to have another day to be alive and write on this page. Lately I've had acid reflux disrupting my life. Although it's been painful, I find it humorous. I've been trying to ignore what my soul has been telling me. My body won't let me ignore it! I've had to dig deep, come to grips with what my soul has been telling me, and then take action to change it.

Thought for the Day:

I listen to my soul's whispers.

I Am Beautiful

September 6

I am beautiful. Peeling the layers of my own soul has not been an easy task. It has been very painful at times. It has required me to look at myself for who I know I am. Not trying to be what someone else has said I am. It has at times, forced me to have difficult conversations and stand up for myself. It has also made me curl up in fetal position and sob. I am someone who refuses to be anything but who I am.

Thought for the Day:

I am proud to be me.

I Am Beautiful

September 7

I am beautiful. What a cool, gentle morning. I am so grateful to be alive. I re-read something this morning that's been on my wall since it inspired me. "You attract what you think. Your thoughts attract unto you like a magnet". –Abraham-Hicks

Thought for the Day:

I am healthy and prosperous.

I Am Beautiful

September 8

I am beautiful. What a lovely September morning. The nights are getting cooler and the days are too. I am so grateful I have another day to do my healing work.

Thought for the Day:

I am happy, healthy, safe and free.

I Am Beautiful

September 9

I am beautiful. What a misty morning in the mountains! It is foggy outside, cool, and so magical. The days are getting shorter. They are still hot, but the nights are getting colder. Fall is definitely on its way.

Thought for the Day:

I am happy and content.

I Am Beautiful

September 10

I am beautiful. Transitions... As the days transition from summer to fall, I feel myself transitioning too. I know as I change in the littlest ways, I am changing for the better.

Thought for the Day:

I am kind and loving.

I Am Beautiful

September 11

I am beautiful. Some trees are beginning to turn. The smell of autumn is in the air. The days are getting cooler little by little. The days are getting shorter little by little. What a great day to be grateful for all I have.

Thought for the Day:

Everything I do, I do with love.

I Am Beautiful

September 12

I am beautiful. Today is the anniversary of my sister's passing. It's a great day to celebrate her life and what she brought to mine. I miss her being physically here, yes, but I know that whenever I want to connect with her all I need to do is think of her.

Thought for the Day:

I celebrate the beauty of life.

I Am Beautiful

September 13

I am beautiful. Today is a great day to be alive. More than ever it is important to go within myself. It is important for me today to realize that whatever I do to another, I do to myself. I am not separate from anything else on this planet.

Thought for the Day:

I am kind, loving, and thoughtful.

I Am Beautiful

September 14

I am beautiful. What a lovely cool morning! The birds are singing; the air is crisp; the sky is blue. I am so grateful for this day. I want the world to be a gentle place where people love and care for one another. Not just physically, but emotionally too.

Thought for the Day:

I behave the way I want the world to be.

I Am Beautiful

September 15

I am beautiful. I follow the "law of attraction" (Abraham-Hicks) today and pay attention to what I want to attract. I want to attract good people into my life. I want to attract peaceful, loving situations.

Thought for the Day:

I am happy, helpful, loving, safe and free.

I Am Beautiful

September 16

I am beautiful. Today I am grateful for time; time with myself, with those I love. Today is a gift and I will behave every moment as if I remember this.

Thought for the Day:

Today is a gift.

I Am Beautiful

September 17

I am beautiful. I am who I am, and I am proud of myself. What a great day to be alive. I have my routine for beginning my morning. Today I will include something new; another acknowledgement of gratitude before I get out of bed; a new morning affirmation. I will include this every day from now on.

Thought for the Day:

I breathe in possibility and breathe out motivation.

I Am Beautiful

September 18

I am beautiful. What a lovely morning to be alive. The sun is shining. The birds are talking to each other. Across the street, leaves on the tree are illumined by the sun. I sit by my waterfall and listen to water trickle over rocks. I'm incredibly grateful for this day.

Thought for the Day:

I am the Love and Light of God/Higher Power manifested.

I Am Beautiful

September 19

I am beautiful. As I sit outside this morning, I am grateful to be here and be alive. The sun shines on my Cosmos flowers lighting their petals with translucent beauty.

Thought for the Day:

Life is a gift.

I Am Beautiful

September 20

I am beautiful. Another incredible day to be here. The temperature is perfect this morning with a warm breeze blowing. Birds are singing. Moths are flying. The wind feels like change is in the air.

Thought for the Day:

I am love. I share love. I behave with love.

I Am Beautiful

September 21

I am beautiful. Today I celebrate Fall Equinox. The earth is once again in transition. It's time to get ourselves ready for transition too. This is the end of the harvesting season and the start of the resting one.

Thought for the Day:

I allow myself to feel beautiful and grounded in the cycle of the earth.

I Am Beautiful

September 22

I am beautiful. The sky was so beautiful this morning. The treetops were reflecting the brilliant pink-orange color of the sun as it was shining through the clouds. More and more trees are beginning to turn as they are starting to shut down for the upcoming winter.

Thought for the Day:

I have steady abundance during this time of transition.

I Am Beautiful

September 23

I am beautiful. First day of autumn for this year– and it actually feels like it. It's crisp and sunny. The cool air brings a freshness to the day. It's a lovely day.

Thought for the Day:

I am love and joy.

I Am Beautiful

September 24

I am beautiful. I woke this morning to the sound of rain. What a peaceful, gentle sound it was. I am so thankful I have a place to live where I can enjoy the rain in a warm, dry house. Like rain washing leaves on the plants to clean them, I wash myself and let go of things no longer serving me.

Thought for the Day:

I invite in the new as I detach with love from the old.
– Doreen Virtue

I Am Beautiful

September 25

I am beautiful. Today is a gorgeous day; the sky is clear, sun is shining, temperature is perfect and there is a slight breeze. I couldn't have created a more beautiful day if I did it myself. One of the best things is, I don't have control over the day. All I have control over is what I do, think and say. I have control over how I feel about myself. I choose to feel beautiful. I choose to feel empowered and make myself a better person. I choose to love who I am in spite of anyone else in the world. I choose to love others in spite of what they have done.

Thought for the Day:

I am empowered to be a better me.

I Am Beautiful

September 26

I am beautiful. I start today knowing I am an incredible person. Everything I do today, will be to benefit those around me, without expecting anything in return. I will look for people who need help in some way.

Thought for the Day:

I choose to find ways to serve.

I Am Beautiful

September 27

I am beautiful. What an incredible morning; my cats play in the tall flowers as the sun shines and birds sing and talk to each other. As I sit by my waterfall, I am grateful for the gift of time I have today.

Thought for the Day:

Time is precious and I use it wisely.

I Am Beautiful

September 28

I am beautiful. My friends are precious to me. I received a gift in the mail today with a card. It was from two friends of mine, a couple. It was a "just thinking about you" gesture. It made me feel loved making my heart feel good. It's amazing how something so little can brighten someone's day so much.

Thought for the Day:

I give gifts of kind words and actions.

I Am Beautiful

September 29

I am beautiful. I woke this morning to the sound of a flock of geese honking -- on their way to a warmer place. The thought of how they're organized and how they follow their intuition brings a question to my mind. What if we, the people, followed our intuition as easily as other animals do? How would things be different? Just a thought... Nature is amazing.

Thought for the Day:

I open my inner self to be guided by my intuition.

I Am Beautiful

September 30

I am beautiful. I am love. Today I saw a movie called *Feast of Love*. It was another reminder of living in each moment without fear – giving every day your best shot. I came out of that movie crying and smiling; crying for the heartaches we all endure, smiling for the beauty present in daily kindnesses.

Thought for the Day:

I look for opportunities to be kind.

October

October 1

I am beautiful. Today is a great day to be alive - and what a wonderful start to October; leaves are changing more rapidly, a chill is in the air and the sun brings a welcomed warmth.

Thought for the Day:

I am loving and kind.

I Am Beautiful

October 2

I am beautiful. The sun is shining on the treetops, wind is blowing and it's refreshing outside. A new day and new month to bring a good attitude into the world. That's what I'll focus on today.

Thought for the Day:

Good things happen to me every day.

I Am Beautiful

October 3

I am beautiful. Fall seems to be in full force now. Trees are turning, leaves are falling and the moon is still up in the mornings. What a sight to see! It is waning now, getting smaller every day. Last week it was full – a peaceful, bright vision in the sky.

Thought for the Day:

I look for the positive in myself and others.

I Am Beautiful

October 4

I am beautiful. What a great day to be alive! The smell of fall is so sweet. The leaves are beautiful, sun is bright, and the birds are a rowdy bunch. When I pulled my *"Trust Your Vibes"* card today by Sonia Choquette, I pulled *"Pray."*

Thought for the Day:

My heart is open and at peace as I pray.

I Am Beautiful

October 5

I am beautiful. Life is so amazing when I listen to my inner voice. I love how my day unfolds; sometimes smoothly, sometimes jagged, but always a treat if I let it unfold with my inner guidance.

Thought for the Day:

I pay attention, listen and trust my inner Self.

I Am Beautiful

October 6

I am beautiful. Life is so interesting. Today was a beautiful, sunny, not too warm day. I spent the day with a friend being creative, lighthearted, playful and joyful. We had our Saturday lunch together, supporting a local Indian restaurant. We then bounced around town together. I am so grateful to have a friend like her.

Thought for the Day:

I am grateful for my friendships, may they always be true.

I Am Beautiful

October 7

I am beautiful. I received a delicious box of organic vegetables today from a friend. They are locally grown, she receives them once a week, and she shares them with me on occasion. Not only are the vegetables a blessing, but my friend is as well. It feels so good to think about where the vegetables come from; the earth and growers, then from my friend.

Thought for the Day:

I am blessed with earth's bounty.

I Am Beautiful

October 8

I am beautiful. Beauty of the trees – ahhhh- Those that have changed color, next to those that haven't changed yet, is just spectacular. The bright yellows against the dark greens, wow! And an amazing part of it, is that I don't even have to leave my own city to see this. I can just look around at the beauty that's right here. The trees are such a concrete reminder of how we all go through our own changes.

Thought for the Day:

I open to the beauty of my changes.

I Am Beautiful

October 9

I am beautiful. If someone were to ask me about myself, what would I say? Would I talk about who I am as a person? Would I talk about my passion? Would I only talk about superficial things? What is the thing I love to do most in the world? Am I doing it?

Thought for the Day:

I am pleased to be myself.

I Am Beautiful

October 10

I am beautiful. Brrrrr... what a chilly morning. Fall is most certainly here. Bugs are behaving differently, so are people. Days are getting shorter, nights longer. Nesting time for cold weather has begun. It's truly a time to be grateful for what you have.

Thought for the Day:

I have many gifts and treat everyone and everything with love.

I Am Beautiful

October 11

I am beautiful. I have my heart in everything I do. I put forth 100% effort. When I have to do something that isn't in my heart, I feel bad. So I choose to do that which feels good, that which is in my heart. I believe that doing too much of what you love is better than not doing what you love at all.

Thought for the Day:

I honor my passion. I follow my heart.

I Am Beautiful

October 12

I am beautiful. What I love the most is amazing and precious. For me, it's my children-- human and animal. I have such an urge to protect them from harm; knowing they all have their own path to take and lessons to learn. It's sometimes painful to watch them learn lessons the hard way. Yet I know the way they learn, is their way.

Thought for the Day:

I am strong, flexible and willing to let go.

I Am Beautiful

October 13

I am beautiful. And I will live today with this knowing in my heart. I won't let my thoughts tell me anything different.

Thought for the Day:

I live my beauty.

I Am Beautiful

October 14

I am beautiful. How I feel about myself is reflected in my actions. Today I will behave with the understanding that I am beautiful and you are beautiful. We are all beautiful in our own way.

Thought for the Day:

I see beauty in all things.

I Am Beautiful

October 15

I am beautiful. This world is an amazing place. It is full of beauty and love, if that is what you choose to see. It's everywhere. It doesn't mean you pretend the icky doesn't exist, it does. It's just that what you choose to focus on, you create. –Abraham-Hicks

Thought for the Day:

I choose to see the beauty throughout my day.

I Am Beautiful

October 16

I am beautiful. My children are so precious to me. As does everyone parent, I've done the best I could at any moment with what I knew at that time. Today I will focus on loving myself. Even though, there are things I've done I'm not proud of.

Thought for the Day:

I forgive myself for my mistakes.

I Am Beautiful

October 17

I am beautiful. My friends are amazing. When I have heartache they are there with hugs and helping words. I can't imagine going through life without them. I haven't always had good friends. I've had to work hard to cultivate friendships with people who are good for me.

Thought for the Day:

I reach out to those who need a kind word.

I Am Beautiful

October 18

I am beautiful. Last night I went to my daughter's choir concert; my how she's matured- her voice, her body, her attitude. It is so much fun to watch her grow into a woman.

Thought for the Day:

I keep my eyes open to the beauty of others.

I Am Beautiful

October 19

I am beautiful. I love the sky in late October; the boldness of the sunsets and sunrises, the clouds and how they capture color of the sun, and the orange moon and white stars. I went to a friend's photo exhibit last night and was reminded what a gift it is to capture the beauty of nature on film so others may see it.

Thought for the Day:

I am grateful for others' gifts.

I Am Beautiful

October 20

I am beautiful. This morning, I went to a man's house. He reminded me of Willy Wonka. His house is one creative idea after another, and not in the modern sense of creativity. He has taken things other people throw away and made them into something else; like 3-inch diameter ball bearings. He has made these into his kitchen floor. He has made unique stones into his bathing tubs. And it goes on... It was so inspiring for me to see how other people see beauty.

Thought for the Day:

I am grateful for people different than me.

I Am Beautiful

October 21

I am beautiful. I awoke to the first snow of the season; incredible large wet flakes raining down in my yard. And now, the sky is blue with golden leaves quaking in the sunlight on Aspen across the street. It's breathtaking. A day like this makes me happy to be alive, no matter what else is going on in my life.

Thought for the Day:

I have a happy and grateful attitude.

I Am Beautiful

October 22

I am beautiful. I went outside to do some cleanup in my yard. I know the ground will freeze soon, so I want my hands in the dirt one more time before it does. Putting my hands in the soil brings me such peace. I love my solitude; just me and the earth.

Thought for the Day:

I live what brings me peace.

I Am Beautiful

October 23

I am beautiful. It's amazing how difficult it is to be a parent. Becoming a parent is the easy part, but being one is the hard part. I'm not sure I would have listened anyway, if anyone had told me how hard it is. The urge for being a mom was so strong in me. I wouldn't change my past for anything.

Thought for the Day:

I am blessed with all aspects of life.

I Am Beautiful

October 24

I am beautiful. For me, life is this incredible spiral. As I make turns around it, I come to the same vertical place yet "one rung" up. I have a chance to reflect on my new spot and re-invent myself if I choose.

Thought for the Day:

I reflect on where and who I am.

I Am Beautiful

October 25

I am beautiful. It's pretty outside with leaves still on some trees, clinging to the end of life. I am so grateful for another day to see them blow in the breeze. I look at my Crabapple tree's fruit; small, red, clinging tightly to their branches. I know these will help feed the birds in the approaching winter.

Thought for the Day:

I observe blessings in the little things.

I Am Beautiful

October 26

I am beautiful. I've seen an owl on a couple walks this week. They are really amazing birds. There are so many different meanings of the owl; some fearful, some magical. In the book *Animal Speak* by Ted Andrews, there are eight pages devoted to them. I believe I've been seeing them this week because I'm being asked to sharpen my listening and trust in my inner thoughts and inner vision.

Thought for the Day:

I trust myself and listen to my inner voice.

I Am Beautiful

October 27

I am beautiful. What a great day to take stock of where I need more self-discipline. I've decided to make a list of where I think I need to do work on myself. I've put numbers by my list in order of priority. This way, I stop "shoulding" on myself and start doing; a little at a time. I've gone back through my list just to make sure it wasn't a list of "shoulds," but a list of "want to's."

Thought for the Day:

I act with self-discipline.

I Am Beautiful

October 28

I am beautiful. It is a clear blue sky day with birds singing. Days like today make me feel so good about being alive. When I walk in the sunshine with a breeze on my face, I feel happy. It's important for me to take note of things that make me feel happy, and keep those things in my life.

Thought for the Day:

I am more beautiful when I'm happy.

I Am Beautiful

October 29

I am beautiful. Today is my volunteer day. I volunteer once a week for two hours. I love this day because it gives me a chance to give back to my community. When my kids were little, I spent time volunteering in their schools. Now I spend time with the developmentally disabled. It's such a great feeling knowing that I make a difference in someone's life.

Thought for the Day:

I share my time freely.

I Am Beautiful

October 30

I am beautiful. I enjoy walking this time of year; the sound of dried leaves crunching under my footsteps, the smell of decaying leaves. It's a magical transition. This part of the world slowly goes to sleep. It's a time of reflection and gratitude for the gifts from the earth.

Thought for the Day:

I am happy, healthy and thankful.

I Am Beautiful

October 31

I am beautiful. All Hallows Eve day... Halloween day. This is a day celebrated, yet do we remember why? It's a day where the veil between the world of the living and the world of the dead is thinner. It is the Eve of the day set aside to honor our dead. It's a good day for being present in that knowing.

Thought for the Day:

I am aware and honor the thinner veil between worlds.

November

November 1

I am beautiful. This day in the United States is our All Hallows day. A day set apart as sacred; a holy day to honor our dead. This was our original Memorial Day. It's important to honor those who came before us. They helped make the world what it is today.

Thought for the Day:

I reflect on those who came before me. I walk with reverence in their honor.

I Am Beautiful

November 2

I am beautiful. Today I will see the beauty of trees. I will look at one leaf and see the incredible art that is Nature. I will give thanks for the gift of trees.

Thought for the Day:

I see beauty in my life and share it freely with others.

I Am Beautiful

November 3

I am beautiful. I give myself all I need. I allow myself to feel good about who I am. I will not compare myself to others today.

Thought for the Day:

I am proud of who I am.

I Am Beautiful

November 4

I am beautiful. Today I will live compassion. I will be aware of not only the suffering of others, but of myself. I will open my heart to letting go of my pain and thereby giving myself permission to be happy and content.

Thought for the Day:

I let go of pain and forgive myself for holding onto it.

I Am Beautiful

November 5

I am beautiful. Today I will hold my head up high, shoulders down in all my interactions. I will remember to breathe and have confidence in myself. I will behave as if I am worthy of goodness in my life.

Thought for the Day:

I am Love, Light and worthy of all good things.

I Am Beautiful

November 6

I am beautiful. I look in the mirror today with gentleness in my eyes. I smile at myself and see beauty lighten up my whole face.

Thought for the Day:

I am the beauty I am.

I Am Beautiful

November 7

I am beautiful. Today I will do something nice for someone else and not let them know who it was. I will find beauty within me by the kind things I do.

Thought for the Day:

I feel special by helping someone else feel special.

I Am Beautiful

November 8

I am beautiful. I will not judge myself today. I will look in the mirror, smile and compliment myself. I will be aware of the fact that as I quit judging myself, I will quit judging others.

Thought for the Day:

I am OK as I am in this moment.

I Am Beautiful

November 9

I am beautiful. Take a deep breath in through your nose and out through your mouth. I want you to make another list of 10 things you like about yourself; just like you did on March 5th. After you write it, I want you to look at the 1st list from March. How far have you come in learning to love yourself?

Thought for the Day:

I am gentle with my precious Self.

I Am Beautiful

November 10

I am beautiful. Today is sunny, cool, and windy. I watch the trees move in the wind like dancing seaweed in water. They are graceful and lovely. Their movements remind me to keep moving myself; to keep flexible in this ever-changing world.

Thought for the Day:

I am loving and flexible.

I Am Beautiful

November 11

I am beautiful. What a great day to have your thoughts in alignment with what you desire. Today's date is 11/11. That means your thoughts are manifesting into form. – Doreen Virtue

Thought for the Day:

I keep my thoughts in line with what I want.

I Am Beautiful

November 12

I am beautiful. It's easy to judge another. The hard part is to see yourself in the person being judged. When I catch myself starting to judge, I look at the person or situation with love in my eyes and heart. I silently say, "God bless this person."

Thought for the Day:

I practice not judging others by not judging myself.

I Am Beautiful

November 13

I am beautiful. Today I'm going to be conscious of being conscious. – Eckhart Tolle What does this mean? I will pay attention/be aware of the space between my thoughts; my breath, my silent stillness.

Thought for the Day:

I pay attention to my breath. I take slow conscious breaths.

November 14

I am beautiful. Another great day to be alive; to see the world around me with open eyes and an open heart. Today I will focus on being an observer of myself.

Thought for the Day:

I watch my body and my thoughts as if I am outside of myself.

I Am Beautiful

November 15

I am beautiful. I am remembering the flowers. They come up and give us their scent and their beauty without ever asking for anything in return. They pop up, live as fully as they can, and then pass.

Thought for the Day:

I live as richly as a flower. I share my love and beauty with all I come in contact.

I Am Beautiful

November 16

I am beautiful. As I read this, I am fully aware of my presence. I feel my bottom in the chair. I feel my eyes move from left to right. I feel myself swallow and blink.

Thought for the Day:

I take time throughout my day to be aware of the present moment.

I Am Beautiful

November 17

I am beautiful. As I pay attention today to the present moment, I won't judge it. I will accept things as they are without labeling them as good or bad.

Thought for the Day:

I accept this moment fully as it is.

I Am Beautiful

November 18

I am beautiful. It seems the closer I get to a goal, the harder it becomes to finish it. I know, though, that I can do whatever I put my focus on. So, today, I put my focus on being in the moment and completing a task without being sidetracked.

Thought for the Day:

I pay attention to getting something completed one second at a time. I know that my day is made up of "seconds."

I Am Beautiful

November 19

I am beautiful. It's amazing to me how busy we can all get. When I catch myself telling someone I "don't have time", I stop and reassess. Time is the only thing we really do have. When I stop to take a breath and realize the only time is now, I relax and feel my aliveness within me. It's a beautiful thing.

Thought for the Day:

I take many moments in time today to pay attention to my breathing and feel life flow through me.

I Am Beautiful

November 20

I am beautiful. I finished a two-day class today on suicide intervention. During class, I remembered something that's been taking place for over a year now. I am changing into the person I am, not who I think people want me to be. It feels good to be alive in my own skin.

Thought for the Day:

I am the inner me that no one can see.

I Am Beautiful

November 21

I am beautiful. Today feels like one of my favorite places; windy, cool, rainy... It's a place where I feel most at home; like where I came from. I am grateful to have this moment on this day.

Thought for the Day:

I appreciate everything about this day.

I Am Beautiful

November 22

I am beautiful. Numbers are powerful things in our lives. Today is 11-22. In Doreen Virtue's Book, <u>Healing with the Angels</u>, she says this about 1's and 2's: "Your thoughts are like seeds that are beginning to sprout... These are signs that things will and are growing in your aspired direction. Keep the faith!"

Thought for the Day:

I pay attention to my thoughts. I focus on what I want to bring into being.

I Am Beautiful

November 23

I am beautiful. Today I will pay attention to my body. I will feel my body at different times during the day. Not just my outer body, but my inner body. I will feel the aliveness inside myself.

Thought for the Day:

I take deep breaths and feel the stillness within myself.

I Am Beautiful

November 24

I am beautiful. I went through a journal of mine today; one that I started two years ago. It's amazing what I learn about myself and the process of my life when I keep records of it. I recommend keeping a journal to anyone.

Thought for the Day:

I reflect on the things I've learned.

I Am Beautiful

November 25

I am beautiful. Every day is a new day. Every day is a brand new start. Today I will live as if it's the first day on this planet. I will see each situation as it is; a new situation.

Thought for the Day:

I learn new things about myself.

I Am Beautiful

November 26

I am beautiful. After reading the first part of Elizabeth Gilbert's book, _Eat Pray Love_, I am reminded to incorporate more pleasure into my life. So I'll make a list of things that make my heart sing. Now, I'm going to pick one of those things to do today that will bring a smile to my heart.

Thought for the Day:

I sit in moments that bring me pleasure.

I Am Beautiful

November 27

I am beautiful. My teenage daughter complains about my friends. How they are "weird." But I have found that life is more fun when you diversify the people you hang out with.

Thought for the Day:

I cherish everything in my life; the people, plants and animals.

I Am Beautiful

November 28

I am beautiful. I have a much better day when I notice amazing little things. Like watching birds come to the feeder in my backyard. They are different colors and beautiful. I am so grateful I have my eyesight so I may see details on their little bodies. They are truly magical.

Thought for the Day:

I pay attention to little things that make my day special.

I Am Beautiful

November 29

I am beautiful. I close my eyes and take a deep breath. I notice the smells in the room. I hear the subtle sounds. I pause. What I notice is life inside and outside myself. I feel alive and vibrant. I've decided to have a great day; just today, just now. Not paying attention to the past and not worrying about the future.

Thought for the Day:

I remember to breathe and pause to feel alive.

I Am Beautiful

November 30

I am beautiful. The scent of pine wafts through the air. Dang, I love that fragrance. It reminds me of my childhood, winter and anticipation. It reminds me who I am; that I am beautiful inside and out. It reminds me that I'm not alone and have help wherever I go.

Thought for the Day:

I find things everywhere for which I am grateful.

December

December 1

I am beautiful. What an incredible day to be alive. The mountains are so beautiful today. They are deep purple with white and lighter purple clouds above them. Today I will focus on not only seeing beauty in the world, but those around me as well.

Thought for the Day:

I love myself and others around me.

I Am Beautiful

December 2

I am beautiful. I am so grateful to have this day. This is a great day to spend some time with friends - talk, laugh, connect. The sun is shining. There is a chill in the air making it feel so fresh.

Thought for the Day:

I share myself with my friends. I give the gift of time and listening.

I Am Beautiful

December 3

I am beautiful. It's a fabulous day to spend time fixing up my space. I will intentionally make it cozier today. I will clean out clutter that has accumulated over the year. I will seal the one window allowing cold air to come through. I will create a "clean slate" so I may start fresh and begin anew.

Thought for the Day:

I embrace my space.

I Am Beautiful

December 4

I am beautiful. Snow. It's magical. It falls from the sky perfectly white. It is so delicate. It can be super soft and light, or soft and heavy. It's a gift. When it snows, it reminds me to relax in what is. Also, how much I don't have control over some things. It makes me grateful for what I have, such as a home in which to stay warm. It makes me grateful for food I have in my refrigerator and cupboards. It helps me remember to pay attention to things over which I do have control. And do something about it, if need be.

Thought for the Day:

I am strong and wonderful.

I Am Beautiful

December 5

I am beautiful. Time is one of the most precious gifts any of us have. We may not think so, but it is. We need to arrange our time to be with people who mean the most to us. How many times have we thought, "I'll do that later"? Well, NOW is the only time there is. NOW is another time's "later". There is a saying in the Tao Te Ching, "Nothing is done and nothing is left undone." Live right now.

Thought for the Day:

I consciously live in each moment.

I Am Beautiful

December 6

I am beautiful. I am beautiful. I am beautiful. The sun is shining today and birds are singing. I love who I am and exercise my body. I feel good and have a smile in my heart.

Thought for the Day:

I listen to the sound that is my own.

I Am Beautiful

December 7

I am beautiful. Birthdays are a great thing to be celebrated; for the mom and the child, even if the child is much older now. The child was and is such a gift to the parents. Also, to celebrate your coming into the world is a joyous occasion. There is no better time than now to appreciate yourself and your life.

Thought for the Day:

I am happy to be alive.

I Am Beautiful

December 8

I am beautiful. This is another great day to be the best me. I look at the world as a place full of love and possibilities. I am full of possibility. I open my eyes and heart to seeing what today holds for me.

Thought for the Day:

I am open to possibilities. I am gentle and loving with myself.

I Am Beautiful

December 9

I am beautiful. I am full of life and grateful. I am relaxed and stress-free. If I notice a thought that makes me stressed, I will look at what I would feel like if I didn't carry the thought with me. –Byron Katie

I will notice how I interact with others and how I treat myself. Today is a day of great awareness.

Thought for the Day:

I let go of stressful thoughts.

I Am Beautiful

December 10

I am beautiful. It's a great day to be alive. I am so thankful to be who I am. It's another day to be the best me I can be. How can I do that? "Pay attention. Take responsibility. Ask questions. Don't assume anything. Don't take things personally."- Don Miguel Ruiz

Thought for the Day:

I am responsible for examining my thoughts.

I Am Beautiful

December 11

I am beautiful. I am happy to be alive and have a place to live on this freezing day. I look in the mirror and don't pass judgment. I see my inner beauty. I know if I love myself then others can love me too.

"Pay attention. Tell the truth without judgment or blame. Don't be attached to outcome." Angeles Arrien

Thought for the Day:

I am free of judgment of myself and others.

I Am Beautiful

December 12

I am beautiful. Snow, snow, beautiful snow -- sparkling in the moonlight. I could sit and watch its subtle colors for hours. It's gentle and magical.

Thought for the Day:

I look at my true beauty, I am a miracle.

I Am Beautiful

December 13

I am beautiful. The squirrels at my feeders are so peaceful to watch. They are very observant. One gets his food and hops up to a higher branch to eat. The other one keeps his eyes on me looking at him through the window. I wonder what he sees.

Thought for the Day:

I observe myself from the outside.

I Am Beautiful

December 14

I am beautiful. I awoke this morning to big beautiful flakes of snow falling again. What a magical way to start the day! This is another day I can practice gratitude for things I have; my legs that walk, my eyes that see, my ears that hear, my mouth and hands that speak.

Thought for the Day:

I am as unique and tender as snowflakes.

I Am Beautiful

December 15

I am beautiful. A child is born. What could be more pure than a newborn baby? How special they are. How delicate. How beautiful. They are a gift.

Thought for the Day:

I am a gift.

I Am Beautiful

December 16

I am beautiful. Animals. Wild and Domestic. They are amazing creations and additions to the world. The animal friends that live in my house bring me much joy. They eat, clean themselves, play and sleep, just as humans do. They let me know when they want attention. They're observant of the world around them and behave differently if something is threatening their domain. They teach me a lot about caring for myself just the way I am.

Thought for the Day:

I love myself and those around me.

I Am Beautiful

December 17

I am beautiful. Intuition. Always there, followed or not. What a blessing are those still small voices that come to me throughout the day. Even if I don't listen, they still come to me, in faith that one day I will listen. I am so grateful for the times I have listened to my intuition. It has never failed me, never been wrong.

Thought for the Day:

I listen to my intuition, that quiet, small voice.

I Am Beautiful

December 18

I am beautiful. The snow is so magical. It can fall gently, with light flakes floating from the sky. It can fall in heavy, rain-like sheets. It is beautiful to watch, however it comes. What amazes me is that every flake is different from every other one. Just like people. Every flake is beautiful in its own way, just like people. When you can look at yourself like you look at a lover, you'll never think bad thoughts about yourself again.

Thought for the Day:

I look at myself like I look at someone I love deeply.

I Am Beautiful

December 19

I am beautiful. I have a job to do, we all do. We all came here for our own purpose. It's up to us to figure out what that is. I came here to help others in every way I can. Others have come here for different reasons.

"Know Thyself" -Thales of Miletus

Thought for the Day:

I open myself to knowing myself.

I Am Beautiful

December 20

I am beautiful. I am in charge of my own day. Whenever I feel that others run my day, I will look at myself in the mirror and remember this is my life and I make decisions for myself.

Thought for the Day:

I am powerful I. I treat myself lovingly and with respect.

I Am Beautiful

December 21

I am beautiful. Winter Solstice. Today I'll be grateful for the Sun and the Moon, the day and the night. It's the longest night of the year and the beginning of longer days ahead. It's a great day to hunker down and focus on the positive.

Thought for the Day:

I keep my thoughts on what I want.

I Am Beautiful

December 22

I am beautiful. Living life is what being alive is all about; to not sweat the small stuff is an art. It's easy to pay attention to details and forget to look at the big picture. Today I will focus on the big picture. I am beautiful inside and out. I am a living human being who cares about the world around me.

Thought for the Day:

I am loving and at peace.

I Am Beautiful

December 23

I am beautiful. Today I will remember to treat myself lovingly and with respect. I will gently remind myself that I am a beautiful person and deserve love and respect from me as well as from others.

Thought for the Day:

I am gentle and loving with myself and others.

I Am Beautiful

December 24

I am beautiful. Today, as I opened my eyes, I said thank you for another day to be me. I then went to the living room and stretched. I started my day slowly, with reverence for myself. It feels good to honor myself. I will also honor myself today by putting nutritious food into my body and positive thoughts into my mind.

Thought for the Day:

I am consciously gentle with my beautiful self.

I Am Beautiful

December 25

I am beautiful. If you step outside early this morning, you'll feel a peace in the air. Outside, the world is quiet; nobody rushing to work, no engines rumbling. It's calm. Since today is a day of gift giving, why not give a gift to yourself – a gift of peace – step outside early, if only for a moment.

Thought for the Day:

I honor my peace within.

I Am Beautiful

December 26

I am beautiful. It's a great day to be alive. Today I will have a quiet day. I will start the day with ten minutes of breathing and calm. I will go to my favorite spot in the house or outside, close my eyes and focus on my breath.

If I just can't seem to carve out the time, I will be gentle with myself and do this tonight as I lay in bed.

Thought for the Day:

I slowly breathe in through my nose and out through my mouth.

I Am Beautiful

December 27

I am beautiful. I am thankful for the gift of another day. Today I will pay attention to my mood. If I catch myself being grumpy, I will check in with myself and see if I am HUNGRY, ANGRY, LONELY, or TIRED. Then I will take a deep breath and respond to what I've discovered.

Thought for the Day:

I nurture myself in whatever way I need.

I Am Beautiful

December 28

I am beautiful. Today is a day full of wonder; the sun is shining, clouds are floating, birds are singing and I am breathing in and out. I can see. I can walk. It is truly a day to be thankful for all that I have and all that I am.

If I catch myself using a negative thought toward myself or others, I will stop, take a deep breath, and look for the beauty.

Thought for the Day:

I see beauty everywhere I look.

I Am Beautiful

December 29

I am beautiful. Have you ever stopped to feel the wind on your face? How did it feel? Was it warm and gentle? Or was it cold and harsh? Next time it's a windy day, stop to really feel it. Really notice whether or not you push against it, or relax and feel it.

Thought for the Day:

I allow the elements to touch my skin and the sun to kiss my face.

I Am Beautiful

December 30

I am beautiful. I love my body. I feel good in my skin. Today I will practice loving my physical body. It's perfect just the way it is.

If this doesn't feel true, then say it a few more times. This is the only body you have; treat it with love, compassion and respect. If you don't like it, then start today to make a change so that you do like it.

Thought for the Day:

I love and embrace everything about my body.

I Am Beautiful

December 31

I am beautiful. Today is a good day to reflect on the past year. What did I do that made me feel good in my body, mind and spirit? What did I do that made me feel bad? I will look through last year's journal entries and calendars. I will make time to write down my findings and write what I want next year to look like. I will journal with the intention of learning from the past so I can make changes and continuations for today and the future.

Thought for the Day:

I am grounded and reflective in my thoughts today.

Resources

Abraham-Hicks. Abraham-Hicks. *Audio recording.* 2007.

Chopra, Deepak. The Spontaneous Fulfillment of Desire. Harmony Books. N.Y. 2003.

Choquette, Sonia. *Trust Your Vibes.* Hay House. Cards. 2004.

Katie, Byron. The Inner Awakening. Simon & Schuster. 2007.

Ruiz, Don Miguel. The Four Agreements. Amber-Allen. 2007.

Tolle, Eckhart. A New Earth. Penguin Group. 2008.

Virtue, Doreen, Ph.D. Healing with the Angels, pg. 161. Hay House. 1999.

Wind, Rev. Margarita. Charted Pathways. Mystic Veil. 2000.

© Shannon Ansted Hake 2012-present

Please feel free to share this as long as you acknowledge where it came from. Nothing in here is intended to prescribe, diagnose or otherwise give medical advice. Please consult your medical practitioner as needed.

www.ingramcontent.com/pod-product-compliance
Lightning Source LLC
LaVergne TN
LVHW052257070426
835507LV00036B/3096